Critical Acclaim for Don Surath

From Training Clients

"I found your seminar very motivating. Practicing your cold-calling skills has paid off. Media Play is now one of our new advertisers. The seminar was helpful, enlightening, and profitable. Thank you."
— Debra L. Seversen, Sales & Marketing Consultant
KSMP, Minneapolis

"Everyone on the sales staff has stopped by my office to thank me for bringing you in."
— Phayne Sherwood, Business Development Director
KBHK TV, San Francisco

"After your seminar in Orlando, our regional directors voted unanimously to have you return and share your wisdom in developing effective business relationships. Your second seminar provided our staff the training necessary for them to be successful. I was heartened to hear their success stories. Thanks again for a job well done."
— Arnold Swope, Deputy Executive Director
America's Charities, Chantilly, Virginia

"After taking Don's "Conquering Cold-Calling Fear" training, I doubled my success rate within one week."
— David Miller, CEO
WorldPantry.com, Redwood Shores, CA

From Supervisors

"Don is a real asset. I know I can count on him making his sales quotas every month. I wish I had ten of him!"
— David McGahey, Local Sales Manager
KFRC AM, San Francisco

"You have topped your sales goals consistently. Your positive attitude permeated the entire staff. When some new change happened at our startup network, you accepted it and made it work for you. Thanks again for being there whenever I needed you."
— Mauricio Mendez, General Manager KKPX TV, Redwood City

"Don has once again demonstrated that he is a major part of the KKSF sales force. His new-business performance is the highlight of both the fourth quarter and the year, setting a new-business billing record. What stands out is his ability and willingness to help others, by providing leadership, contributing to sales training and meetings, and generally being a team player."
— David Kendrick, General Manager
KKSF FM, San Francisco

From Sales Clients

"Don is the best rep in this business. Thank you for placing him on Western's account."
— Linda Taing, Media Buyer
Western International Media, Los Angeles

"Thanks for a job well done on our behalf. We've been at PAX TV for four months now and are seeing a huge increase in our Yellow Page response. Since we've done nothing else different, we attribute the increase to your channel."
— Barbara Cunningham
County Consumer Plumbing Service and Repair Group,
Redwood City, CA

"My client, Codiroli Car Company did a last-minute buy that your sales rep Don Surath structured. Don did a great job explaining the benefits of KABL AM and then made sure all the spots ran properly. The results were astonishing! In two days we sold 35 new and a dozen used cars. As a result of Don's structure, planning, and hard work, we think you have a new long-term client."

— Bud Fitzsimmons, Compass/West Advertising

"We booked thirty markets with Don Surath last year and have been pleased with the quality service and attention our agency receives from him. Without Don handling our account, we would probably not spend what we do with PAX TV."

— John Graziano, President
Max Media, San Juan Capistrano, California

"I have been lucky enough to work with Don Surath during the past five years. Don is more than a familiar voice on the telephone. A few years back, he and his family took time out of a vacation to visit us in South Carolina. We've maintained a great relationship ever since. Had it not been for that, I don't believe I would have ever sought out PAX TV."

— Carolyn Stafford
Richmond Advertising, Pawleys Island, South Carolina

"... our associates will be more successful."

— Eric Yale Lutz
Lutz Capital Corp., Detroit, Michigan

"I can truly say that Don is a rare find and a joy to work with. He knows his product, and is willing to go the extra mile to make sure my advertising is effective and make me feel like a valuable client."

— Kim Groce, Marketing Director
Tanforan Park Shopping Center, San Bruno, California

Conquering
Cold–Calling
Fear

Before and After the Sale

Don Surath

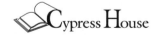
Cypress House

Conquering Cold-Calling Fear ~ Before and After the Sale
Copyright ©2003 by Don Surath

Cypress House
155 Cypress Street
Fort Bragg, California 95437
(707) 964-9520
Fax: 707-964-7531
http:\\www.cypresshouse.com

Library of Congress Cataloging-in-Publication Data
Surath, Don, date-
Conquering cold-calling fear before and after the sale / Don Surath.
    p. cm.
Includes bibliographical references.
ISBN 1-879384-50-7 (paper : alk. paper)
1. Telephone selling. 2. Selling. I. Title.
HF5438.3 .S87 2002
658.8'4--dc21   2002011090

Book production by Cypress House
Printed in Canada
2   4   6   8   9   7   5   3
First edition

Acknowledgments

One of the best parts of writing *Conquering Cold-Calling Fear* was the chance to reconnect with many past and current friends and associates who were instrumental in helping fashion my sales-training career.

Let me start by acknowledging my true love and life partner, Susana Sanchez. For the eleven months I was working on my book, she worked hard at Colsky Media with hardly a peep about why I didn't get a real job. It was only when we started to fight the dogs for their dinner that she finally put her foot down and asked nicely if it might be time for me to find full-time employment.

Susana also added her editing comments to those of my sister-in-law, Tania Sanchez, who edits the in-house magazine at New York Life. Tania's first comment was, "Not another fifty-year-old salesman telling the world how he did it!" Reading her candid comments on the first draft, I felt she had nailed it. A couple of months of brooding later, I took her advice and did a massive rewrite that I hope meets her approval.

There are sales managers who influenced me in more ways than they will ever know. Margot Falzerano gave me my first job in radio sales, with the promise that if I brought in new business she would take care of me. She introduced me to Anthony Robbins' training before the world knew his name, and taught me the coffeecake call you'll read about later. I paid attention and quickly grew to be a star for her. Margot is the best closer I've ever met. She's also the only person who hired me twice, the second time for my first sales-training position at the Chris Craft TV station group.

The late David McGahey, my next manager and one of the nicest people who ever walked the Earth, turned me on to the Jason Jennings technique of radio sales, and wrote a reference letter that has helped me snare several sales positions.

Joe Cariffe, to whom I lost a job at KKSF, turned my bitterness around at once, and also taught me how to raise prices, sell to auto dealers, and create the car-dealer pitch that got me hired to sell TV time by a manager who'd already decided on someone else.

Harry Friedman was the retail-sales trainer who started my belief in sales training. He made it possible for me to look at an unknown Anthony Robbins with an open mind, practice the Jason Jennings technique to great success, and make lots of money using Dr. Philip LeNoble's System 21™. If you read the book, Harry, give me a call.

First, Paul Karasik, and especially June Davidson, of the American Seminar Leaders Association, pounded into my head that I must write a book; it would never have happened without them. Thanks as well to June's associate and a constant source of encouragement, Alina Pogaceanu, and my co-university members who worked with me to set goals and learn technique, and provided moral support. Thanks to Stuart Bardach for moral support, Joan Foder for tactical help, Josette Allen and Betsy Sawyer for help with publicity and logistical assistance.

When one starts out in sales, other staff salespeople are often suspicious and guarded with their support. Not Samantha Spivak. As a co-worker she was generous with her support, and has remained my strongest booster for more than a decade. She arranged my first sales-training seminar, designed my first brochure, and worked with me in both radio and TV, ever ready to sing my praises.

How about those City Feet gals, Sheri Swank, Jan Nuttall, and Gillian Ellenby. This book started out to be a business biography.

After finishing a first draft with lots of help from three former ace City Feet managers, I realized that the general interest level in my life was not extremely high. The many laughs and reminiscences were a highlight of my writing experience.

Thanks to Carmen Rutlen whose success in being published in *Chicken Soup for the Soul* gave me hope that I could do it, too.

Justin Herman helped with the website and designed the phone men. Thanks to Stuart Bardach for constant moral support.

After I'd put the book down for six months, Paula Glaser, who's employed at my favorite camera shop, encouraged me to finish writing it. I went home that day, completed the last few chapters, and sent it to the publisher. Thanks, Paula, for the kick in the pants I needed to complete the task.

My daughter, Marlo, the best girl in the whole world, had the benefit of my participation in her budding basketball career at Gateway High School while I wrote the book. She was embarrassed when I showed up at school to help the auction committee, but her grades and attitude were exemplary during this period. Marlo will do great things someday.

I'd better not forget the staff of four at my lovely 1626 Noe Street home office. They were cooperative, friendly, always supportive, affectionate, and protective of my privacy. Ellie Mae Sanchez, Lara Bea Surath, Eddie Munster, and Iggy Pup were awesome. Ellie Mae, a red cairn terrier, likes to sit on my lap every afternoon about three. Lara, a lovely, sixty-pound charcoal gray GSP/Lab mix, wants to go outside after breakfast. Eddie, a black cat who adopted us one Friday the thirteenth, enjoys walking on the iMAC keys and meowing to go out. Iggy, the largest American Eskimo on earth, lets me know when people walk by, and likes to sleep at my feet under the desk. A guy couldn't ask for a better working group.

Many others influenced me; some are mentioned by name in the book. Special hellos to nephews Randy and Adam Genser;

niece Leslie Surath; cousins Harvey, Bonnie, Lewis, Hannah, John and Lisa Foreman; Diane Scher, Rachelle and Roy Volger, Vivian and Bob Curry, Steve, Nicki, and Julie Maimes, Ken Disner, Nancy, Jack, Lori, Kevin and Vicki Shapiro, Dr. Carl and Shirley Schwartz, Annie, Carey, Jesse and Daniel Austin, Jesse, Ann, Diana and Felica Sanchez. If I left anyone out, I'm sure I'll hear about it soon.

Finally, there is my loving mother, Rose Surath. My dad, M. H. Surath, used to refer to her as "The best mudder in the New Nited States." Pop's been gone for twenty-two years now, but his assessment is still perfect. Just the thought that I have the sweetest mom gives me the strength to finish what I start.

When I was eighteen, I decided to hitchhike from Detroit to New York to visit my older cousin, Diane. She was living an artist's life in the East Village, hanging out with a not-yet-famous Bob Dylan. When I told my mom of the hitchhike plan, she offered to drive me to Telegraph and Seven Mile Road at 5 A.M. to start my journey. As she let me off, she told me she had always wanted to do something daring like that but never had. I was living her dream.

We never fight. We always get along through heartache and joy. My mom. My hero.

In Memory Forever

Morris Surath

Alice Surath

Harold Surath

Lee Genser

Introduction

While selling computer systems during the 1980s, I kept an appointment with the owner of a large hardware store. He had a small office adjacent to the stockroom. As I set foot in the office the guy held up one finger and said, "One word."

His meaning was clear: If I said the right word, he'd spend some time listening to my pitch. The wrong word meant I was outta there.

Think about it for a minute. What would you have said to this ultimate decision-maker? The right word and you can pitch the $40,000 system he needs to help run his business; the wrong word puts you on the street.

I thought for what felt like an eternity, but was probably under a minute, and answered, "Computers."

His answer: "Get out."

For the past fifteen years I've pondered what word would have gotten me a seat in his office. For years I thought something X-rated might have worked—his place had calendars featuring scantily clad models displaying the latest tools.

The quest for that perfect answer has led me to search, figuratively speaking, the four corners of the Earth. My search has uncovered many amazing examples of the right and wrong words to use with prospects in the sales arena. *Conquering Cold-Calling Fear* is an attempt to share those results with you, so *you* never have to face the intimidating hardware storeowner unarmed.

Many of the situations described in *Conquering Cold-Calling Fear* occur during the sale of radio or TV airtime. I cite them to provide a consistent backdrop for teaching winning cold-calling techniques that you can implement in your industry. For optimum results, substitute your field for the ones mentioned here.

What's In It for Me?

What you'll learn in *Conquering Cold-Calling Fear* are *short-cuts* that *absolutely* work to help make your sales life easier and more fun, while achieving greater success than you ever thought possible.

You will master the ability to:

(*Develop an elevator pitch;*

(*Co-opt the dreaded gatekeeper;*

(*Reach the unreachable prospect;*

(*Circumvent voice-mail hell;*

(*Establish rapport* immediately;

(*Simmer down independent business owners;*

(Get *the appointment;*

(*Achieve a positive outcome at* every *face-to-face meeting;*

(*Look forward to every client visit;*

(*Make the "Coffeecake Call" work for you;*

(*Use body language to your advantage;*

(*Be an expert in your prospect's business in a few easy lessons;*

(*Leave the "me" and "our" out of your vocabulary, replacing it with "you" and "your";*

{ *Establish trust;*

{ *Spend less time on your sales pitch while making it more effective;*

{ *Have only nice people for clients;*

{ *Be the person whose phone calls are always answered;*

{ *Always know who is your most important client;*

{ *Make your manager love you;*

{ *Close the deal;*

{ *Keep 'em buying long-term;*

{ *Handle internal selling smartly;*

{ *Avoid having your support staff hate you;*

{ *Collect all your money — on time;*

{ *Use geography to make friends.*

We will learn how to:

{ *Use "The Cancellation Turtle" effectively;*

{ *Overcome bad news;*

{ *Do nothing when in doubt;*

{ *Deal with unreasonable demands from a superior;*

{ *Develop the sweet value of being a ticket broker;*

{ *Kiss the correct asses—correctly;*

{ *Write an effective business letter.*

Who will Benefit
from Effortless Selling?

‹ *Sales managers who want to jump-start their staff;*

‹ *New salespeople who must write business or perish;*

‹ *Fund raisers;*

‹ *Nonprofit development directors;*

‹ *Small business owners;*

‹ *Students trying to influence college admissions officials;*

‹ *Job seekers;*

‹ *Public speakers.*

Contents

Chapter One

Why you should listen to me

If you've been in the business world for any length of time, you've attended company-sponsored seminars. You probably heard the rule of thumb that one good seminar idea put to use makes the event worthwhile, right?

What about the seminars and workshops where you sat and stewed all day as some over-the-hill clown turned out to be a colossal waste of your time?

After sitting through the third workshop given by a full-of-himself has-been who was stealing my time and bushels of my boss' money, it occurred to me that I could do a better job. He was boring our radio station sales staff with name dropping from his halcyon Philadelphia radio days in the 1970s. If you're going to drop names, at least *impress me!* We'd never *heard* of these people.

It was San Francisco in the 90s. An entire sales department sat for three days waiting for some skill we could use to make up for time off the street losing business to our competitors. Instead, we left angry.

For years I taught my sales staffs techniques that made them exponentially better. Why not combine my skills as an educator, years of sales and management experience, and hands-on training techniques from the likes of Tony Robbins, Dr. Philip LeNoble, and Harry Friedman, to help people learn new skills they could use immediately? I thought it possible to teach a more effective seminar than many I'd witnessed.

I wanted to design workshops where participants practiced the techniques they were learning. The workshop would be unsuccessful if participants forgot a skill a week later because they never put it into action. How about learning a technique and then going directly to the phones, trying it out, and coming back for instant feedback?

Business obligations that have piled up, demand instant attention after returning from a seminar. You're soon back to your regular routine. The new skill is a fading memory. The way to own a new skill is to practice and become comfortable with it before you continue your routine. Practicing until you own a new technique is a key premise of my Conquering Cold-Calling Fear Seminars.

Exercise Number One

Take your left hand, place it over your left shoulder, and reach as far as you can toward the middle of you back. Keep it there. Now take your right hand and do the same. Now pat your back ten times with alternative hands.

Congratulations! I can't be there to personally pat you on the back for having the courage, patience, acting ability, and thick skin to be a successful salesperson. You have to do that yourself for now. Only one person in your business life will give you pats on the back — your manager, when you surpass new business quotas, and maybe not even then if your manager is always hard on you.

The rest of the sales staff will like you from time to time, depending on *their* sales figures. If you start with a bang, popularity will be tougher to gain. You'll need courage to withstand backbiting and jealousy. Your toughest competitor isn't someone from a competing business; it's the person in the next office or cubicle.

Then there's your support staff. They rarely salute a person getting twice their salary, plus free parking, who's off doing *who-knows-what* each day. You need them all desperately, so you must be civil. Later, I'll offer you tips on gaining their respect.

Finally there's your client base. When you grasp *Conquering Cold-Calling Fear,* your clients will become both the best part of your job and the folks who pay your wages. Treat them dishonestly and a trusting consultant relationship can turn to dust in an instant.

Let me share with you the experience of many successful years in sales and sales management, where I learned specific techniques that changed me from a salesman to a consultant. If you practice these techniques, you will be more successful, or I'll give you your money back. That's a promise!

Chapter Two

Never forget for a moment your most important client...
Your Boss!

When your manager is happy with your performance, you won't be hurt when a buyer calls with a complaint. Your manager will back you if you're making her look good by bringing in new business.

Conversely, don't think for a minute that because your clients like you, you've become indispensable. When your manager says that new business development is his most important priority and *means* it, having good advertising-agency relationships will not suffice — many people can handle agency business.

Why do you think seasoned Account Executives (AEs) fight so hard for those accounts? It's easier to call on existing accounts than summon the courage to cold call. The agency has already been sold on the station.

Agency selling focuses more on negotiating rates and ratings than performance. AEs have to put up with regular bouts of humiliation from professional buyers used to having the upper hand in relationships. There's more paperwork with agencies, because buyers have to account for every dollar spent. A station's strengths may be ignored in favor of current ratings position. The product becomes a commodity to be traded. The good news is that an AE's income fluctuates less with agency business — so long as ratings are strong.

In the post-merger world of larger station groups, new business becomes more important. The high prices paid for stations mean rapidly rising sales goals. Agencies feel threatened by the new realities and aren't eager to buy more without strong justification. New business generators are becoming crucial to station survival.

New business stars have conquered the fear of cold calling. They will be rewarded with low-paperwork agency accounts that can be profitable and fun. Cold-call specialists can always find work no matter how many times a station is sold and management changed. So hone your skills on these pages. Become your manager's best friend by helping surpass his or her new business budget.

Chapter Three

What You Should Do

Read this part of *Conquering Cold-Calling Fear* with an open mind. There will be sections you think are helpful in your quest to make your selling experience more effective. Other ideas might seem hard to put into action, but don't despair — they'll sharpen your skills if you give them a chance.

Exercise Number Two

Cross your arms. Now switch arm position so your arms now go the opposite way. Feels odd, doesn't it? Cross the new way every time and soon it will become second nature. The original position will be uncomfortable.

You might have been exposed to the folded arms exercise at past seminars. I use it here to demonstrate being open-minded about learning new ways to operate as a salesperson. Try my suggestions for a month. Judge the results for yourself. Let's begin.

Getting Started

Before you start cold calling, take time to prepare the situation. This Friday afternoon, combine ~~leads torn from newspapers, direct mail, magazines, and the *Yellow Pages*~~, with clients you have failed to reach. Enter every business name and phone number onto an Excel spreadsheet. Better yet, ~~if you have~~ a client-tracking

online, on air & Print leads

USE

system like ~~ACT!, or that~~ SALESFORCE. You'll need to record each phone call, names of important contacts, and personal details necessary to better serve your new friends.

Jason Jennings of the Quantum System suggests starting with *100 leads.* I agree. When I did the Jennings training at KFRC AM, I was the only one on the staff to finish my list of 100. My Jennings success far overshadowed the rest of the team. You can start your leads list in one week with no trouble.

If you already have a working list, you probably think that compiling the 100 leads list is too much work. Take the thirty "dogs" from your list and use them as a starting point. Do you want to be the *best* or just middle of the pack? Salespeople do not reach the top and stay there without working harder than everyone else.

Pulitzer Prize winner David Halberstam, in his fascinating biography of Michael Jordan, *Playing for Keeps,* tells what set Michael apart from his peers. Jordan was not satisfied being chosen rookie of the year with the Chicago Bulls. He returned to his alma mater North Carolina and asked mentor and college coach Dean Smith what Michael could do to become a more complete player. Smith said to work on becoming the best defender in the league. Jordan worked on defense the entire off-season, and returned the following year a more complete player.

Michael spent each off-season working on a different aspect of his game. One year it was his jump shot, another year, three-pointers. He never quit until he had six championship rings.

Tiger Woods did a similar thing. After being named *Sports Illustrated* Sportsman of the Year and becoming the youngest player ever to win The Masters Championship, Woods started a weight-training campaign that added fifty pounds of muscle. Next, he totally changed his swing, because he knew he could only be the all-time best with a different swing. By the year 2000, Tiger had the greatest year in golf history, winning eleven tournaments, three major championships, and over $9 million in total earnings.

I mention these sports analogies to drive home the point that if you wish to be number one, you must be an excellent cold caller who can develop new business easily, even with a large agency list.

If you feel you're too busy to compile the 100 leads, try this:

(Collect all the ~~newspaper~~ *PRINT* *ads you've torn out.*
✦ Research Websites
(*Find phone numbers you have meant to call.* **20 CALLS A day**

(*Look through your stack of business cards.*

(*Pick up the largest daily and weekly local papers.*

(*Check the* Yellow Pages *for plumbers.*

You can find 100 names in no time.

(*Put them in a pile on your desk.*

(*Pick a night this week to stay late.*

(*Enter them in your contact file or Excel spreadsheet*

(*Give the list to your manager to verify (you'll probably lose ten, so find a few more).*

Now you're ready to start. You'll never have to do this again at your current station. Those 100 cold leads will be enough to keep you busy for a long time.

My rule of measurement is *a minimum of twenty calls a day.* Fewer than that will not yield the critical mass necessary to generate enough appointments. You can close the book now if you promise to make twenty calls a day every day of your sales career — and *keep* the promise.

It's amazing how lucky you'll become when you make twenty calls a day. Often, people who were thinking they needed to buy but weren't sure whose services to use will be on the other end of the phone. New hires, who don't have built-in prejudices, as well as buyers frustrated with your lazy competitors, are waiting at this *instant* to take your call.

Charm, wit, and good looks will lose out to the twenty-calls-a-day person every time. Try 100 calls in five days next week and see if I'm correct. I predict at least seven appointments and two sales without reading another line of this book. For instruction on how to turn those 100 calls into thirty appointments and ten sales, read on.

Chapter Four

Your Elevator Pitch

What do you say when someone you meet in an elevator wants to know about you? You have about thirty seconds to make an impression before the elevator hits the ground. Your goal in this chapter is to develop that "elevator pitch" so you can make an instant impression whenever you meet someone.

June Davidson, of the American Seminar Leaders Association, teaches the proper way to let people know what you can do for them. Instead of saying, "I teach seminars on cold calling," start with a problem that you solve as part of your job:

"You know how salespeople have a hard time picking up the phone to make those cold calls?"

Stop and wait for your listener to either nod or speak in agreement. It's great if they add a few examples or confide that as their biggest fear. You've grabbed their attention and induced them to acknowledge the problem. Now go for the grabber:

"Well, I teach people how to conquer that fear."

That entire pitch took fifteen seconds. I stated a problem, established its credibility, and provided the solution. The value of such a succinct pitch is multifaceted: you've introduced yourself, probed to find whether there's need for your services, and wasted practically no precious time.

A conversation mate who's interested in your services can take it from there. If he's not, fine, ask him what he does. Remember, the less you say about yourself and the quicker you turn the conversation over to him or her, the more you'll be appreciated.

Soon you'll start making calls. Most often someone other than the ultimate decision-maker will take the call. That gives you time to perfect your elevator pitch, which must be ready on the off chance that the decision-maker happens to answer the phone and wants to get to the point of your call.

More about that technique soon, but let's try a couple more scenarios. Let's say you sell janitorial supplies. Instead of saying, "I sell janitorial supplies," how about:

"You know that stale smell in some restaurants and public buildings? Well, I consult with building managers to find effective ways to eliminate those smells."

That's a big improvement. Now take out a piece of paper and write your elevator pitch. Write it first, then practice in front of the mirror until you're comfortable with how it sounds. Remember, no more than twenty seconds! Don't read another word until you've written your elevator pitch and practiced it a few times.

Now comes the test. The best place to try it out is a party or mixer. I first constructed my elevator pitch in the winter and then tried it out at a Christmas party. It was hard at the beginning, but after saying my pitch a few times it became easier. Before I left the party. I had secured a new client.

The man had an online business that relied on garnering new partners through cold calling. He was great at the technical end, but his business wasn't taking off because he lacked cold-calling skills. He is now an ongoing client whose business is growing exponentially.

A short problem-solving elevator pitch will give you instant credibility, increase your confidence, and make you money. What are you waiting for? Develop it now!

Chapter Five

Picking Up the Phone

Your confidence level has already risen; now it's time to pick up the phone. Be ready to enter the information you're about to gather quickly. The answers will come fast. Have your contact file open to the first name on your list. If you still write, have enough writing materials close at hand so as to not waste anyone's time by having them repeat names and numbers while they face a buzzing switchboard.

Your first goal in making your calls is to find out who is the ultimate decision-maker. Practice using a direct approach. Pick up the phone and call the first number on your list. Paul Karasik asks:

"I wonder if you can help me out?

Wait for the answer:

"I hope so. What's your question?"

Everybody loves to be helpful. Now ask:

"Who makes the business buying decisions at this organization?"

You've asked an easy question. The receptionist is relieved to be able to be helpful. When you are given the name, say thanks and ask his or her name as pleasantly as possible.

"And may I ask your name too?"

Many times, the gatekeeper answers the phone by saying:

"XYZ Company. Marlo speaking."

Be ready to enter that name at once. If you miss it, stop immediately and have her repeat her name. If it's an odd one, have her spell it for you. Wow — someone who cares!

Enter the names, thank the operator, and hang up! If she asks whether you wish to speak to the person, resist temptation and say you're only gathering information.

Sorry, no sales pitch today. Wasn't that easy? Do you think you can power through the 100 names in a few days doing it that way?

Sometimes the operator either doesn't know or is forbidden to divulge the information. In that case ask:

"How would someone go about finding that information?"

If he repeats the original refrain, he is *fogging* you, and you'll never get the information from him.

Fogging is a term we used in my shoe stores to keep undeserving customers from getting refunds on shoes they'd bought, worn to parties, and brought back a few days later. When such people asked for refunds, we merely repeated our written policy of no refunds, and gave them options of another pair of shoes or a store credit. If they persisted, we repeated the policy again in exactly the same tone. Soon realizing there was no choice but take one of the offered options, they did.

That's what happens with businesses that don't want decision-makers bothered by sales pests. A gatekeeper politely continues to say the decision-maker is not available. Eventually the salesperson gives up and goes after other prospects. The good news is, when you do reach such an insulated decision-maker, you'll be one of the lucky few and have a better chance of success.

When you're convinced the person who answers the phone will never reveal the info you want, be sure to get *his or her* name and hang up. When you eventually find the decision-maker, you'll still have to deal with this previously unhelpful person, so you might as well have one of the pieces of the puzzle in place.

There are two solid ways to secure the answer you seek. The first is the random directory search. Most businesses have employee directories. If you're lucky, names and titles will appear. When you encounter names only, pick out someone who sounds interesting and call *him*. Chances are, someone who doesn't get many calls will answer and be willing to talk.

Ask your question the same way as before but add:

"I've been floating around in your phone system looking for the marketing director. Can you give me a hint on the name and number?"

Fishing works best when you reach someone in research. Their job is to help. You've asked a simple question that they're fully prepared to answer. While you're at it, ask about the Web site — you might need to find your decision-maker through it if you strike out everywhere else.

Web sites are great sources of information. Even if your guy is listed with no number, you can now access him through the phone directory when you're ready. See? It's almost impossible to fail when you have a plan.

Decision-maker Answers Phone

Occasionally, the decision-maker answers the phone. Great, talk to her. Tell her whom you represent and ask:

"When is a good time to find out if your business is a match for our station?"

If the prospect presses you to reveal what you're selling, merely say:

"There'll be plenty of time to talk about my station. What's important now is to find out if there's a fit. The only way to do that is to learn about your business first, because I don't know if my station is right for you yet."

Try again to set a meeting by letting her know you'll be in the area on Tuesday and could fit her in either before 10 A.M. or after

1 P.M. You must be prepared: it's impossible to know when opportunity will present itself, and a blubbering response at your first encounter will be exceedingly difficult to overcome.

Back to the introduction calls. We ask you to find only names on the first call for two reasons. First, to become comfortable asking a simple question in a direct manner. Many inexperienced salespeople are afraid to ask a direct question for fear of rejection. Using a direct approach 100 times will cure most folks of that fear. Getting used to saying exactly whom you represent is liberating. When you reach a decision-maker with a direct introduction, you know he or she is in some way interested.

The second reason for getting names only is that on Wednesday through Friday, when you call the decision-maker, you'll sound like someone who is *sure* he's going to reach that party. Now you know both the decision-maker and gatekeeper. This valuable information gives you a huge advantage over other cold callers.

Chapter Six

Making the Gatekeeper Your New Best Friend

If you think the gatekeeper's not important, get up out of your chair and go over to your receptionist. Ask Roz what percentage of callers asks for her name. You'll find that about *five percent* ask. Then ask what she thinks of the people who address her by name. You'll find she takes extra care to give those calls special handling.

Need I say more? The receptionist is the company's gatekeeper. She has the worst job at the lowest pay in the organization. People treat her as if she's nothing but a hindrance to their holy mission. If you've ever been in that position, you know how it feels to be treated like dirt by 95 percent of the people who call. When a knight in shining armor calls and asks about your vacation or kids, it can turn your day around. You can be sure that person's call will get special attention!

Most sales courses talk about *getting by the gatekeeper or by-passing the gatekeeper*. As long as you retain that attitude, you'll never be fully effective. Why not make a new friend today? It feels great to say something to a person and have him or her reply, "You made my *day*!"

From now on, that will become part of your job. See how many *days* you can make each day. Isn't that better than trying to outsmart people all the time?

The point made *ad nauseam* here is:

Let's have fun helping businesses make more money.

Each sales job I've taken has been easier than the one before. Part of the reason is that I use the techniques I'm sharing with you to make gatekeepers *my new best friends*. They love to take my calls and help out whenever possible.

The easiest way to become the gatekeeper's special friend is to ask questions. Start by asking simple ones, like:

"How's the weather in Seattle today?"

"How long have you worked at XYZ Company?"

"Is XYZ company a fun place to work?"

Now listen carefully to the answers. One-word answers show indifference, experience, or someone in a hurry. When that happens, say:

"You sound swamped. Is there a better time to call?"

That usually works. People like it when you acknowledge the importance of their positions. You will also know when *not* to call next time.

You'll usually get an answer to one of the first three questions. Use that answer as a stepping stones to establishing a relationship. Please be flexible. Listen to what is said and use it.

Meet an answer like:

"This heat is unbearable."

With a probing:

"Really — have you set any records?"

"What was the temperature today?"

"Does your air-conditioning work?

"Do you have air conditioning?"

The answers can lead in many different directions.

You've hit pay dirt when the gatekeeper shares *anything* of a personal nature at this time. Think of yourself as a fisherman who has just hooked a fish. Take the probe in the personal direction from which it was directed.

"It's so hot, I'm worried about my daughter after school."
Should be followed immediately with:
"How old is yours? I have a six-year-old."

Once the topic of kids is broached, it's easy to form a common bond. Often, the gatekeeper is young and inexperienced. Maybe no one at the office cares about her problems. By becoming the one person who cares, you'll strengthen your relationship with the gatekeeper.

You're building a foundation of trust with the gatekeeper while doing something positive. Being friendly is its own reward. If you never make a dime from this person's company, you've still done a good deed by brightening up her day. You'll feel good whenever you hang up the phone after one of these calls. People are often lonely. You've made an effort to cut through the daily drudgery of someone's life. That's a good thing!

Some experienced gatekeepers will see through your attempts to engage them in conversation. They might make fun of you to others in the office when you're off the phone. Who cares? Being considerate is its own reward. Do it!

Chapter Seven

Surviving Voice-mail Hell

Buttering up the gatekeeper is a great idea if there *is* a gatekeeper. What happens when you hit voice mail and can't reach a live person to perform all your newfound magic tricks? What can be done to short-circuit the voice-mail maze?

Patience is one of the top virtues of successful salespeople. Listen to the messages. Some still say:

"If you have a rotary phone stay on the line and someone will be with you."

Stay on the phone!

Sometimes, you'll hear about the company directory. Pick a number, any number. When transferred to voice mail, listen for that person's assistant. Instead of leaving a message, push the assistant's button. Usually, if the assistant is busy, he can direct you to the operator. If not, leave a message for the assistant. His job is to screen calls. Your message will be returned and you will now be in possession of a most important name.

Winning Over the Personal Assistant

The personal assistant to a major decision-maker is the classic gatekeeper. He or she is savvier than the receptionist, and has endured an incredible number of sales pitches. Don't be surprised if you have to use several methods to gain the assistant's confidence.

The assistant is not as lonely as the receptionist, has many important tasks to complete, and occupies a position of authority in the business. Often the assistant is the *"no"* person in the organization, screening offers for the decision-maker. You might have to speak more quickly to gather the information you need. The assistant often wants you to identify yourself before passing you through to the boss or even giving out the boss' name.

You have 100 calls to make, so leave the message and move on. You need to make contact with an assistant of some kind first. Plus, you don't know the decision-maker's name yet. Leave no message for the decision-maker. That's O.K., you're dealing in large numbers here. By the time you've made twenty or thirty more calls, the assistant will call you back.

Remember: leave only your name and phone number for the assistant. There'll be plenty of time to let a decision-maker know the nature of your business. That time is *later.* The assistant needs to only know enough to return your call. When he or she finally calls you back, use the same technique you used with the gatekeeper:

"I wonder if you can help me out?"

Then wait for a response. Again the usual response is:

"I don't know if I can, but I'll try."

Now he has committed to trying to help you. Then you say:

"I've been having a hard time negotiating your voice-mail system. How do I find whoever makes the final decision to buy advertising?"

You'll almost always get the answer you seek using the "Can You Help Me?" method. Now you're talking to the assistant/gatekeeper and you say:

"It's tough to get through your voice mail — can you give me any tips that'll shortcut the process?"

If you've done your due diligence with the assistant, this part will go smoothly. She won't give away company secrets to someone she doesn't trust. If you fail to engage her, chances are the information trail ends with:

"What is your name, name of your company, and nature of your business? I'll leave a message for Ms. Decision-maker to get back to you."

That response equals failure. The decision-maker will never return your call, *and* will be alerted that you're a pest she never wants to meet. Your best bet when someone is about to blow your cover is to say you're being paged and hang up. Get off the phone before divulging any more information. The great thing about bailing out is, the gatekeeper/assistant will forget you as soon as the next call comes in. To insure a clean slate, make a note in your contact file to wait a couple of days before trying again.

Listen to the assistant's language pattern. If he or she speaks quickly, speed up your speech pattern. With slow speakers, never rush. Try to sound as much like them on the phone as possible. When you call from New York to Mississippi, there are two strikes against you unless you understand this crucial lesson. Slow down!

Check your contact file. Correct greeting technique will get you the decision-maker's extension. Continue gathering names until the gatekeeper column is also full. Patience… patience. Your success increases with proper preparation.

I don't pretend to know all the answers (O.K., maybe I do). You might have a phrase or technique I never use. While you're thinking about the process, e-mail me: **yfds@pacbell.net**, and your tip will be included in our Web site.

Voice mail has never been an impediment to me, because every business day there are human beings working who answer the phone when it rings. Today, thanks to the Internet, voice mail isn't the end of the line. Almost all companies list their marketing departments on their Web sites. You might find both the decision-maker and assistant's name there.

No access to the Internet where you work? Take those tough-to-find names home and research them at night. You may be able to call the decision-maker directly as a result of your search, and worry about the gatekeeper later.

No Internet access at all? Subscribe today. You can't be successful in the twenty-first century without it.

You can use an e-mail address to contact the company CEO first. Ask the CEO who makes the decisions on advertising. She might give you her underling's phone number. When you call the advertising decision-maker, you can honestly say the CEO told you to call. Those calls get returned!

Chapter Eight

Reaching Decision-makers

The importance of knowing gatekeepers will become evident when you try to reach decision-makers. Upon calling, don't say:

"May I speak to Judy Rubin please?"

That's a sure way to be given the "Name, company, nature of business" grilling. Instead, try:

"Hi Denise. Is Judy in?"

Since you haven't talked to Denise in a couple of days, she probably won't remember that you called on Monday to ask both her name and who made the buying decisions. Denise might figure you're a regular caller and patch you right through, but don't count on it. An experienced gatekeeper has heard that trick before and will still ask you to identify yourself. With not a second's hesitation, start with your full name:

"Oh sure. It's Julie Rodovan."

Sometimes, you'll get away with only your name if you say it in a quick, casual way. A sharp gatekeeper is going to ask the name of your company. Again, don't hesitate. Give it to her.

As soon as you show fear, the gatekeeper will shut the gate with you permanently outside. If you're afraid to try this method, start with your worst prospects. You'll have little to lose. After a few rough calls, it'll be time for the important ones.

It usually takes at least two calls to reach a decision-maker. When the first call yields voice mail or a "She's not in right now," leave a message like this:

"Hi, Judy. This is Julie Radovan. I have a couple of questions I was hoping you could help me with concerning the XYZ Company. I'll try to reach you later today or tomorrow, depending on my schedule. Thanks."

Don't ask Judy to call you back — she never will. Waiting for a callback will be the end of the conversation, with you waiting by the phone forever. It's safe to assume that a new prospect will seldom call you back. Why open yourself to failure? Take charge of the situation by letting prospects know you'll keep trying until you reach them.

My rule for reaching new prospects is, *call twice a day for three days.* If you call once a week you'll never be remembered. Six calls in three days will pique anybody's attention. Your name will become embedded in his mind. A prospect will often take your call out of curiosity. If that person has any sales background, he'll respect persistence.

If you fail after the third day, revisit your new best friend, the gatekeeper. Explain your difficulty in reaching the prospect, and ask for hints on how best to reach this obviously busy and important figure. Would the decision-maker object to e-mail? If you've established a stronger relationship on each call, the gatekeeper will tell you if e-mail is appropriate. Use e-mail sparingly unless it's the industry norm.

Sometimes, the gatekeeper will walk into the prospect's office and implore the decision-maker to "talk to that nice young woman, Julie Radovan. From today on, you need to work with the gatekeeper to insure becoming that fortunate person. The tactics you used with the receptionist must now continue with the personal assistant. Work that person. Get to know him.

Contact by E-mail

E-mail is becoming a huge part of every business today. The job-search business has adopted e-mail as the initial contact medium of choice. It's well accepted in Internet sales, and was incredibly successful in the 1990s when the medium was new and folks didn't walk into work every day with fifteen to fifty e-mails waiting for an answer.

With virus warnings, SPAM, and corporate spying on personal e-mail clogging up systems, - is no longer a guaranteed way to earn a quick response. My friends who fled radio and TV during the Dot-com gold gush of 1999–2000 found after a while that they had to use the phone to reach decision-makers.

When sending e-mail, the key element is the *Subject Line*. What will make the decision-maker open your e-mail? Think of what works for you. If you're working for a recognizable station, mention it in the Subject Line. A TV question might work — more people respond to TV than radio.

A straightforward approach can work best. Since you've been trying to reach the decision-maker for a few days, your name will be familiar. He might figure e-mail is the safest way to find out what's on your mind. When he opens your e-mail, it had better be powerful. If not, he'll never answer your call, because he'll have already made a negative decision.

E-mail is an incredibly versatile tool we use daily. It works best when a phone contact has already been made to start forging a sales relationship.

Web Browsing

Web browsing is a great sales-research tool. Use it every day for locating hard-to-find addresses. Download logos for your presentations. Ask for information, and a salesperson might call. That will give you a chance to ask your opening question of a person who's not a gatekeeper. I have fantastic success using this tool.

The Fax Machine

I had a client who ran a large consumer-electronics-advertising department, and was practically impossible to reach by phone. Janet, her assistant, and I had become good friends, so she offered tips on when to call. The company didn't have e-mail, so I couldn't reach Bernadette that way. My only hope was exercising my writing skills on the fax machine.

Bernadette had a teenage daughter who was a handful, so my fax spoke to a quest for advice on how to handle *my* fifteen-year-old daughter's first boyfriend experience. I mentioned nothing about my TV network.

A couple of hours later, a call came through, with a thoroughly amused, hard-to-reach client on the other end. My fax worked, an appointment was set, and a pitch could be made.

Most people read their faxes. Whether they'll respond depends on both your writing talent and the number of faxes they have to wade through daily. Use the fax machine as a last resort. Use it to send requested information to current clients. Try not to fall into the trap of faxing info instead of earning an appointment.

When you can't reach the prospect by phone, you'll rarely earn enough respect to start a financial relationship. Also, you don't want to give the decision-maker the opening to have you fax all proposals. Face to face is your goal.

The phone is almost always your most powerful tool. When your manager insists that you continue pursuing a prospect, after failing by phone, e-mail, and fax, a personal visit might be necessary.

There's nothing wrong with dropping in on someone who's been impossible to reach any other way. Bring something for the gatekeeper, and say you were in the area and wanted to meet her in person. Then ask if she'll buzz the boss. If the decision-maker still refuses to see you, ask if there's a better time to return and make the appointment. If, by chance, you're ushered in, keep the meeting brief and to the point of setting a time for a future visit.

If these suggestions don't yield success with a particular prospect, put him aside for now. You have ninety-nine others to work. Come back to the tough ones later, once you've achieved initial success elsewhere.

By all means, record the days and times in your contact file. Don't be paranoid about somebody reading it. The first thing you should do in the morning is log on to your contacts. Start where you left off yesterday and review whom you must call today. The only way to keep track is to enter the data. If you're still writing, go through your prospect book and do the same.

After a couple of days, your appointment book will start to fill and other duties will have to be managed. Make the twenty calls by 10 or 11 A.M., and you'll have the rest of the day for appointments, meetings, and writing proposals. The only caution is Monday morning between 8 and 11 A.M. Buyers hate being bothered then — they're overwhelmed with the week ahead, and generally not in great spirits.

Many sales teams have meetings Monday mornings anyway, so that particular problem might be moot at your station.

Solving the Phone-Tag Problem

Everyone has had phone-tag frustrations. What if you get your prospect on the phone briefly? He says:

"I want to talk with you but I'm tied up right now, Can you call back tomorrow?"

If you can't convince him to take five minutes right now, and you find tomorrow has turned into a week or ten days without a connection, call back your new best friend the gatekeeper and say:

"Jim said he wanted to talk with me but we've been having terrible phone tag problems, can you check his schedule and see if he has a few minutes next Tuesday at two?"

If the answer is positive, have her pencil you in for that time. Then add:

"Let Jim know about the appointment. If there's any problem, either Jim or you can call me back. We're all so busy these days, this is probably a better bet."

Don't try this tactic without a solid relationship with the gatekeeper! I scheduled myself to successfully close a large radio station consultancy not too long ago. When I arrived for the meeting, there was absolutely no discussion of how I'd managed to be there. The sales manager respected my ability to get the appointment.

The appointment could not have been arranged without a strong gatekeeper relationship. The manager was too busy to return calls, but relied on his assistant's good judgment and gave him the authority to make the appointment.

I treated that gatekeeper with respect and he trusted me in return. Try the tactic with someone you've established a good relationship with, and see how it works. You'll be surprised how much easier your job will become. After you succeed, go back to other gatekeepers and reestablish relations to get them on your team.

Chapter Nine

She's on the Phone —
What Do I Say Now?

When you finally get the decision-maker on the phone, that person becomes a prospect. Your goal is to size up the prospect as quickly as possible without having her hang up on you. The most efficient way is to start audible mirroring. Anthony Robbins teaches the technique. It works.

Listen carefully to the prospect's voice and voice patterns. If she is speaking quickly, speed up your pace to mirror hers. For slow speech, slow down. The rule here is, *people like people who are like them.* The sooner they perceive you in that light, the quicker you'll break down barriers on your way to become a consultant.

For fast talkers, the best way to slow them down is to get them to talk about themselves. When someone says:

"I'm in a hurry I can't talk now."

Do not say:

"I'll call you some other time."

Neither should you give a sixty-second sales pitch without taking a breath. Acknowledge the person's state of mind by asking:

"Really — where are you off to?"

Or:

"Busy Morning?"

Your goal in this first conversation is to have the prospect speak

70 percent of the time. That will never happen with you running your mouth. Besides, you desperately need to qualify the prospect or *your* time will have been wasted. If the prospect doesn't bite on your probing questions about why the rush, say:

"I just called to set up an appointment. Would Thursday at 2:30 be a better time to speak with you? You seem swamped."

Acknowledging the person's pain makes him think about how he's treating you. Often, he'll slow down and agree to talk for five minutes only, expecting to hear a sales pitch.

Don't give him the pitch, I beg of you. Your goal here is to establish yourself as a person who is checking *him* out, not vice versa! What you say once you slow down the procedure is:

"If you don't mind, there'll be plenty of time to talk about my station. What I want to find out now is whether your business is a fit with us. Could you help me out by answering a couple of questions?"

Sales managers warn not to call prospects until you know something about their business. *Reality check!* Salespeople don't have time to do the research. When forced to research before calling, we often just don't call. Probing is important, since you're not going to know enough about the prospect's business. Listen carefully and take notes. Both business and *personal* content are important here. One of the best questions to ask is:

"How did you get started in this business?"

If it's an odd business, like casket wholesaling, there's bound to be a stock story complete with a couple of laugh lines. The question is asked daily, so the answer is rehearsed. For a run-of-the-mill decision-maker, the question isn't asked enough, so he'll often be more than willing to tell his life story.

During the years I bought advertising for my shoe stores, hundreds of salespeople tried to secure my business. I tired quickly of young "suits" telling me their station was number one. Special packages didn't work. I met anything that smacked of the merchandise approach (pushing a product rather than offering a service) with disdain.

What worked was when AEs were smart enough to get me talking about my brilliant marketing strategy, or how I started in the shoe business. I had no peers to share my stories, you see. I was at the top of the pyramid, and couldn't share with the other shoe store owners in town. We hated each other. Much information was off limits to my employees. I went through two wives in the business. Work-related discussions at home did not prove successful.

The only folks who would listen were a few smart AEs. I probably spent way too much on print because of the friendships I developed with the local newspaper reps.

I was bursting with pride at what I'd accomplished at such a young age. AEs smart enough to sit through my stories were often rewarded with a bigger share of my ad budget. *None* of them were radio or TV reps. Print reps either had better training or more time on their hands. They worked me more effectively than electronic-media reps.

There's room for growth here. You need to know that decision-makers are often lonely and in need of someone to share their amazing rags-to-riches tales. As soon as the story begins, you're on your way to securing a face-to-face with the prospect.

What you need to do now is listen for some magic words that secure your place in this person's life. *The moment the prospect mentions anything of a personal nature, stop everything and zone in on the topic.* He or she might say:

"I moved here because my husband was transferred."

The next thing out of your mouth must be:

"Moved? From what part of the country?"

Now you have the opportunity to talk about a person's hometown! You have mined the mother lode. If they came from a place you never heard of, *get out your atlas* and try to find it. What? You don't have an atlas at your desk. Put this book down right now and go to AAA or a State Farm Insurance office and pick up a free USA road atlas.

A former sales associate and I recently met and reminisced with a mutual third-party friend. Nicki told how she constantly overheard me going through my atlas, looking for some client's out-of-the-way hometown. That's right! What she neglected to add was, each time I found some obscure spot on the map, I made someone's day.

An easy way to gain favor with a prospect is to respect her birthplace. It's a politically neutral subject that recalls fond child-hood memories. Guess what? Those fond childhood memories will now be forever associated with your call. Why, this person must be OK if he cares enough about me to get out the atlas and look up Brainerd, Minnesota.

If the hometown memories are bad or unremarkable, keep going until you find something else. Remember the 70/30 Rule. As she continues her soliloquy, keep asking questions. Say nothing about your station yet. If she asks about it, you can give a thirty-second description like:

"KKSF has a Smooth Jazz format that appeals to adults who like listenable music. I'm somewhat like a pimp. I deliver 400,000 yuppies to businesses that are looking for that audience. I can tell you more about it when I come to visit. Right now I just want to find out if a visit will be beneficial to both of us"

Such a response shows that you're not hiding anything. You actually *are* interested in hearing more about the prospect's business. It's also a request for more information.

Sometimes, after hearing that you sell radio advertising, the client will say:

"I tried radio. It didn't work."

Never let that statement go unchallenged. Dr. Philip LeNoble's System 21 lays out the following facts that you must ascertain:

❴ *How long was the schedule? Short schedules work only with huge discounts or going-out-of-business sales.*

❴ *What was the offer? Was it compelling enough to get people to come in?*

❴ *How effective was the commercial? Did it clearly state benefits? Did it have an immediate call to action?*

❴ *What station was used? Was it targeted correctly to their audience?*

❴ *Was the product something that sold well, or was it a dog? Price alone won't make people buy a poor product.*

Often, when the client starts answering these questions, he comes to the realization that maybe the campaign wasn't done correctly. Also, he begins to respect you for asking good questions. With each answer, the prospect is filling in blank spaces, which helps *you* formulate his upcoming media plan.

The most common reason electronic media fail to work is lack of consistency. A great comment here is to explain carefully that, according to a study done by Frank Dance, 75 percent of every advertising message is forgotten in two weeks, and 95 percent is lost after three. Even if the campaign was great (a questionable assumption), it might never have run long enough to succeed.

By showing the prospect you understand more about how advertising works, you continue to boost your credibility. Now is the time for the George Zimmer story:

Several years ago, Zimmer spoke to a radio/TV/Cable group, and shared this technique: in every new market he researches, his agency checks to see whether TV and radio will be cost-effective for The Men's Wearhouse. If the price is prohibitive, George skips the market.

Satisfied with the cost-effectiveness of electronic media, Zimmer enters the market with multiple locations and annual electronic buys. It works exactly the same in Kansas City as in San Francisco — he's always successful. Why? Consistency with electronic media, a great slogan ("I guarantee it.") and a strong offer to the public. He uses newspapers only for his annual January sale, because he knows people look to newspapers for word of sales.

George wondered aloud to the gathering, "Why don't my competitors, the department stores do the same?" While The Men's Wearhouse was flourishing, almost all of his competitors wound up out of business or filing for reorganization, wasting millions of dollars on double truck ads that didn't build their brands. By implication, you can now say to the prospect:

"Wouldn't you like to have your business be like The Men's Wearhouse someday?"

You have piqued the prospect's interest. Now is a good time to go for the appointment. Always have your appointment book or contact file ready to insert your new friend's meeting date. When she asks again about your station, you merely state:

"I have an appointment in your town on Tuesday, December 18th, at 2:00 P.M. I could come by for a brief visit to tell you about my station either before or after that meeting. Would one or three be better for you?"

Nothing bad can come of that question. You're closing in on the appointment.

The client has several possible responses:

"I'm not ready to see you. Why don't you send me a media kit?"

O.K., now you know you're dealing with someone who's accustomed to brushing off media salespeople. Never cave at this point. Any person who won't meet you face to face will be difficult to sell on your station. If you can't close the appointment, you'll never close the sale. When a prospect refuses to see me, I sometimes say:

"You know, I've been in this business twelve years and still have yet to sell anything to anyone who only received a media kit in the mail. I've become superstitious in my old age. Can we try some other method to get you the information?"

Or, if you haven't the guts to say that, say:

"Sure, glad to. What's the best time to drop it off so I know it gets directly into your hands. A busy person like you probably has someone screen your mail. I'd hate to have it thrown away, wasting all that paper. Is Tuesday a good day to bring it by?"

It's possible the prospect might then say:

"Either mail it or forget it."

At this point, you have a decision to make. Either blow the guy off, or say:

"You know, I'm not sure we're a fit. Do you mind if we talk some more to see if it's worth both our whiles to send the packet."

Don't send something that has no chance of succeeding. The client will have more respect for you if you continue probing. Once you agree to send your information, you fall into the category of every other spineless sales pest. Your trial close showed that the prospect wasn't yet ready for a face-to-face. Fine — continue probing!

Now ask the client the questions that will generate concrete information about his or her business. The most important figure is annual sales. If the sales are too low, you can cut the discussion short. Simply say:

"I'm not sure your business is the size to need electronic-media advertising. What's worked for you in the past?"

Finish up the conversation with honest suggestions of alternatives. After all, you *did* say when the call started that you weren't sure there would be a fit. When you think it appropriate, suggest printing flyers or advertising in weekly shoppers.

Before you hang up on an unqualified prospect, ask your new friend if she can suggest a merchant in her field who might need your services. A referral from a small merchant you treat fairly will enhance your stature with his or her business associates.

If the reason you called was seeing the prospect's ad on TV or hearing it on the radio, the probing *must* continue. Resistance to giving annual sales figures is understandable. Overcome it by suggesting a range of dollar figures:

"Would you say your annual sales are over $1 million? $5 Million? $10 Million?"

Dollar-figure queries usually help determine whether the client is a fit while further breaking down barriers. If the conversation is still going well at this point, ask again:

"I'm going to be in the area on Tuesday, anyway; why don't I pop in for ten minutes just to get a look at your operation. I'm amazingly low-key."

If the prospect says:

"You can't come by Tuesday. I won't be here."

You have clinched the appointment! Your possibilities are now almost endless. The next word out of your mouth:

"Where will you be?"

If the answer is "In a meeting," merely say:

"What's a better day for you?"

The prospect is cornered. He or she must offer an alternative date or be incredibly rude. It's almost always the former.

When the alternative date is offered, don't automatically grab for it. Try to change whatever time the prospect proposes. If that doesn't work, say:

"I'll have to move a couple of things. Meeting with you is important. I'll call your assistant, Marlo, as soon as possible and confirm, but for now, let's both pencil in the time. Do you have your calendar?"

The advantage of having his assistant as your new best friend is that she'll take care that this appointment will not be canceled — she wants to meet you!

Once the appointment is secured, immediately send a hand-written thank-you note confirming the appointment. Call Marlo later, and let her know that you'll be coming to visit her in a few days. She'll be excited that you took the time to call.

Chapter Ten

Hitting the Vacation Jackpot

Another great, no — fabulous — scenario happens when, in response to your request for an appointment, the prospect mentions that she'll be out of town on the date you'll be in her area. The next words out of your mouth *must* be:

"Where are you going?"

Never pass this opportunity. It's your best chance to forge a personal bond with the prospect. If she says:

"I'm going to Chicago for a convention."

Answer:

"Have you been there before? It's a great party town. How long will you be gone?"

The idea here is to involve yourself in the prospect's joy as she's looking forward to the trip, or her pain if she isn't. When the client is headed for vacation, you can place her in her exotic locale immediately through your probing questions. If you're lucky enough to have visited the proposed vacation spot, the travel tips you offer will be warmly accepted.

The other beauty of the vacation exchange is, you take the prospect out of his office and virtually place him on the beach. Can you imagine what that does to his frame of mind? If, by chance, you've been to the spot and have photos, the perfect exchange can be forged for your visit upon your prospect's return.

Keep in mind that no one in the office is interested in the prospect's vacation. If he or she is the boss, thirty people are jealous. Upon returning, they will pay lip service to vacation stories and bury the subject as soon as politically possible. Co-workers' jealousy will be based on their having to shoulder additional duties while Mr. Vacationer sips banana daiquiris in Cabo San Lucas.

You will be the only one truly interested in the prospect's vacation stories. He will look forward to your visit for no other reason than finally having someone to share his joy with. You are providing a crucial service. I know — I *was* that boss. Remember the smart AE who listened to my stories and got the lion's share of my business?

Tell your prospect the meeting should be set for one week after he or she returns:

"Be sure to bring the pictures."

Send a handwritten confirmation note that will be waiting upon your vacation buddy's return.

Chapter Eleven

The Coffeecake Call

One morning, Phayne Sherwood, the other AEs at Magic 61, and I sat down to wait for GSM Margot Falzerano's sales meeting to begin. Margot swept in with an enormous coffeecake — enough to feed the whole station.

As she began to cut it, she spun a yarn about how the coffeecake came from "this fabulous bakery in Mill Valley" and she just *had* to share it with us. Then she asked if anyone else had a favorite bakery. Of course, people vied to share their stories of gastronomical delight. The meeting turned into a lovefest.

After about ten minutes, Margot turned to us and said:

"I had you guys eating out of my hand, and you can do the same for your clients. Just bring a cake and start cutting."

The idea blew me away. I became a coffeecake maven that day. A coffeecake answers many questions. First and foremost, *it is an icebreaker*. Your arrival at an appointment with someone you've met on the phone might begin awkwardly. Coffeecake to the rescue! The key technique is to bring in the cake and start cutting, which precludes your prospect's putting it aside, voiding its value.

As you serve the cake, talk about the favorite bakery in your neighborhood:

"There's an old-fashioned bakery in the neighborhood, where women wear blue uniforms and little white hats. The recipes are two generations old, and taste different from what you can buy at Starbucks. Do you have a favorite?"

Now you have the basis of a conversation that will relax the client and teach you great lessons about him or her.

You can learn:

(*Does he like sweets?*

(*Is she willing to share?*

(*Do they accept gratuities?*

My favorite coffeecake success was the time I took one to a Southern California client who was undergoing chemotherapy for cancer. It turned out that the next chemo session, with its accompanying nausea, was about to begin.

The coffeecake I brought would be the last thing Justin could eat before he started the treatment. He was a well-known jeweler with pieces worth thousands of dollars in his store, but that coffeecake was the most valuable item there that day. Our relationship became forged in steel.

If the client says he/she never eats sweets, fine. Just say, "If your staff is anything like ours, we can put the cake out where they can reach it and it'll be gone before we finish our meeting."

Many trainees are skeptical of the coffeecake's value. Remember what I said about acting? If you're reading this and saying to yourself, "There's no way I'm lugging in a coffeecake and going through that whole ritual!"

Try the cake once and see what happens. No one will die. You might make a new friend. To be successful in new business development, you must think better. Try the cake!

O.K., it doesn't have to be coffeecake — any baked goods will do. The idea is to break the ice. It almost always works. If you feel uncomfortable bringing a coffeecake, try bringing three items: something chocolate, something sweet, like Danish, and a savory treat, perhaps a croissant. Take them all out and see which one is chosen. Make a note of the choice for the next visit.

Position the three baked goods by taking them out of the bag and saying:

"I didn't know what you liked so I tried three choices. You pick first. Then I'll take one, and we'll give the other to your assistant" (my new best friend).

I let the assistant know that there'll be something good on the way out in appreciation for all her help earning the appointment.

I actually secured one of my sales positions by using the three-baked-goods routine. At my first interview with Mark Libby, of KOFY TV, I hadn't impressed him as much as I'd hoped to. He wasn't planning to see me again.

I prevailed upon him to give me a second chance, by explaining that first impressions are often misguided in employment interviews. I used second interviews for my shoe-sales candidates after having been fooled a few times. He agreed and asked me to prepare an auto-dealer pitch for our second meeting.

No problem. I called Joe Cariffe, former car salesman, then GSM at KKSF FM, and asked for help. Joe had recently given his troops a seminar on how to sell into dealerships. Glad I made friends with him instead of being a pain in the butt at KKSF. The cliché that this is a small business where you see the same faces coming and going is demonstrated perfectly here. You never know when and old friend — or enemy — will pop up.

I learned the auto pitch, then customized it for Mark Libby Motors. Mark had informed me that Retail Sales Manager (RSM) Marc Artieres would join us for our scheduled meeting. I brought three perfectly designed snacks:

(*1 chocolate brownie;*

(*1 blueberry muffin;*

(*1 plain croissant.*

There was one chance to make the meeting work. Every edge was crucial. I showed up for the 4 P.M. meeting just as they were finishing what they thought was their last interview of the day — Mark had forgotten to write the interview on his calendar, but couldn't refuse with me already in the lobby.

On calls when I know the person isn't excited to see me, I usually don't phone to confirm, because such calls give the prospect a chance to back out.

Upon entering the second-floor conference room, I laid out the pastries with my usual rap about the great bakery near my house. Then I began my automotive pitch, hoping they would take the sweets. It turned out neither interviewer had taken a lunch break and both were starving. I could see them trying to hold back. They too knew what taking my offering would mean.

Ten minutes into one of the best-researched and fully prepared pitches in my career, both men reached for the sweet stuff. They later admitted to being famished after interviewing all day. The ice was broken. Another ten minutes went by before they said:

"Surath, you've spoiled a well-laid plan. We're gonna have to hire you. That was one of the best pitches we've ever seen. And the brownies!"

My reply was:

"Thank you so much, guys. But I can't give you an answer until Monday. I have an interview scheduled with KidStar in Seattle tomorrow, and they're paying. I have to see them."

Libby shot back:

"The offer might not still be there on Monday."

My gutsy reply was:

"I'll have to take that chance. I will say this, though: I like you people and want to work here. It just doesn't make sense not to make that trip."

Whew. What an awesome exchange! I wound up taking the

job at KOFY and starring in new business development for several years. You never know what good things will come with the *Coffeecake Call*.

Chapter Twelve

Establishing Rapport
at First Face to Face

As you're cutting the coffeecake, take a look around the room for clues to your prospect's interests. These are windows into their personalities. Little League pictures and pet photos on the wall tell tales. Ask about the photographs when the time feels right. Avoid interrupting yourself and especially the prospect when she's on a *roll* describing her favorite bakery.

You're conducting an interview; your goal is to leave with an appointment to bring back a perfectly tailored proposal meeting the prospect's needs.

Watch how Larry King does it. Larry refuses to trash his guests. He asks easy questions first, warming them up and calming their fears of being on the air. Soon, they love the fact that they're able to spew their views in front of millions of people. Half the show is over before Larry starts zeroing in with the hardball questions. By this time, the interviewee has had a chance to present his or her agenda, and feels more comfortable answering the tough questions.

The Larry King method worked great on my own radio talk show for many years. Guests were always allowed to state their case first before I asked my tougher questions. Occasionally, a guest with cottonmouth had a hard time expressing himself. When that happened, I went directly to questions about home and family, allowing the frightened guest time to relax. Relaxed guests could continue with what the listeners had tuned in to discover.

Prospects also need a warm-up period. If you come in with a canned pitch touting your station as number one for women ages 35–54 in afternoon drive time, experienced prospects will be turned off. Why not warm them up by starting with slow-pitch-softball questions like:

"How did you get started in this field?"

Or:

"Tell me about your most successful campaign?"

Or:

"I'd love to take a tour of your business. Do you have the time?"

These questions start the conversation positively. Business owners like to tell their life stories. When you place them in storytelling mode, good things are bound to happen.

Stay with a prospect when he's on a roll. I often had a list of thirteen questions on my talk show, only to find that the third one opened a Pandora's box of fascination. The phone lines lit up. We had excitement going for the rest of the hour. The last ten questions never got asked.

Be aware of your interview's dynamics. Go with an exciting topic if it's calming the prospect and allowing you to take control of the meeting. Go as far as that road carries you. Your goal is to gather information — as long as your prospect is talking, you're gathering what you need.

What if the prospect says he or she has no time for any questions? Make an immediate mental note that you either failed to establish a sufficiently strong connection on the phone, or failed to reestablish it upon your arrival at the prospect's office. *Never be intimidated into starting your pitch.* Go over the guidelines you set on the phone, to bring the prospect back to the frame of mind that allowed you to make this visit.

Once that's been reestablished, explain again that there's no way to know if you two will be a match until you know more about his or her business. Then make a STOP sign with your left hand and say:

"I have only a couple more questions about your business, and then I promise to tell you all you need to know about mine."

Remember: Assume the prospect is interested in your station or he wouldn't have invited you to take up precious time. Do you think *he* fails to qualify prospects for his business? Ask:

"How do you qualify leads?"

You might find yourself back in autobiography land.

The longer it takes to get to a pitch, the better chance it has of succeeding.

Let your interview flow. Try to spend twenty-five minutes of each half-hour listening. When your prospect is talking, you're inching closer to a sale.

Chapter Thirteen

Mirroring

Earlier, I mentioned holding up your left hand during a discussion, because that nonverbal cue is more powerful than merely saying, "I was almost finished with my questions." Most people recognize the hand-up sign as meaning "Hold on a minute — I'm almost finished." Studies by the American Seminar Leaders Association (ASLA) show that 55 percent of all information is taken in visually. That's why the left-hand STOP sign is so powerful.

The following techniques used properly will give you a powerful tool with which to control any face-to-face meeting with a client. Salespeople who fail to mirror clients often do so out of a reluctance to *act*. The best salespeople are brilliant actors. Come on, now, loosen up and try mirroring.

Anthony Robbins taught me mirroring in 1988 at his "Unlimited Power" seminar, the day *after* he empowered me to walk over hot coals. He was using the technique called NLP developed by Drs. Richard Bandler and John Grinder at UCLA. In the years I've used the technique, no clients have ever noticed that I was mirroring them. Conversely, salespeople have surely mirrored me during that same period, without my having noticed.

The concept is simple: *People like people who are like themselves.* When you're mirroring someone, he sees your body language as similar to his and is quicker to relate to you.

Here's how it works: Remember when I taught you to mirror the tonality of your prospect's voice over the phone? Using that process, you'll notice three types of people:

Visual: These are folks who have to read things to be convinced. They usually speak rapidly and have no time for idle chitchat. When you talk with them on the phone, they might use phrases like:

"I *see* what you mean."

"I'm *looking* at next Monday for our meeting."

Auditory: These people usually have resonant voices, and vary their pitch, tone, and intensity appropriately. They're good listeners, because they respond best to auditory stimulation. For example:

"I *hear* you."

"That *sounds* like a good idea."

Kinesthetic: This group must feel and touch everything. They speak more slowly, wear natural-fiber clothing, and give hugs regularly. Their typical responses would be:

"This meeting next week *feels* right."

"I was *touched* by your offer."

Hopefully, during your phone conversation you discovered the type of person you were about to meet. Guess each prospect's type during that contact. Knowing how prospects will react gives you an advantage in the meeting; you'll go into the meeting acting in a manner that complements your prospect.

Visual people will study your proposal. If they talk fast, pick up the pace.

Auditory folks want to hear everything. Bringing in a tape for them would be great. One successful technique in radio is to write a script and have a strong DJ cut a "spec spot." Hearing a tape evokes the kind of visceral reaction you want. Auditory individuals will relate to you because you understood how important sound is to their comprehending your ideas.

Kinesthetic people will take up a lot of your time. They're in no hurry. They have to feel that you're the right person to work with, so slow down the pace. When you talk, use frequent hand motions. Never try to rush them. Because they'll be the most interested in getting to know you, they're good candidates for business lunches.

As soon as you sit down, notice your prospect's body language. The worst case is someone with both arms and legs crossed, one of the crossed arms folded in front, and the other hand covering the mouth. Such people are entirely closed off to any new information. Your goal is to open them up.

The way to change body language is to mirror your prospect. If he's closed up, you must be too. This is an acting lesson. Prospects never catch you. Start the conversation totally closed and see what happens. After a while, the prospect will feel uncomfortable and want to change positions. Follow suit. After several switches of position, you'll see his arms uncross and the comfort level increase. He's starting to see you as someone like him, because your body movements are similar.

The reason people don't notice you mirroring them is they aren't thinking about you. People are self-absorbed; they care how *they* look and sound. Remember: *People like people who are like them.* You turn yourself into someone like your prospect without uttering a word. It's magic!

You've probably used mirroring and didn't even know it. Watch two people meet in a bar: as soon they discover a mutual attraction, they turn toward each other and start mirroring furiously. The guy says he likes long walks in the park; the gal enthuses about how she loves sports. All the while, they send nonverbal mirroring clues of sexual attraction. Each wants the other to think they have much in common.

You want to convey that closeness — minus any sexual innuendo — by mirroring your prospect, which is most successfully done silently. When you've established rapport by using mirroring, you'll notice at once, by paying attention to body language, if you've done or said something that isn't well received. Changes in body language happen when the prospect senses that he or she has let this meeting go on long enough. The arms that have been in the lap or on the table come up and cross again. Time to make your pitch for a closing meeting and leave.

In an interview in *Modern Maturity,* Ted Koppel says that of all the people he interviewed, Bill Clinton was the best at reading his interviewer and editing himself in mid-sentence. By merely reading his interrogator's body language, President Clinton always saved himself from the big gaffe. Think about it. Every president has famous dumb statements that come back to haunt him, except Clinton. ("I did not have sexual relations with that woman" was not dumb — it was calculated.) Nonverbal communication is the key.

Also, consider President Clinton's background. He came up the hard way in Hope, Arkansas. Bill Clinton was always the man on the make. He *had* to master every skill imaginable to reach the top. Both George Bush and Al Gore were children of privilege. Nonverbal skills were never part of their skill sets. It was less important for them to read people, because neither had to struggle to reach the top. Look at the difference.

Still skeptical about mirroring? Try it out at home first. Practice with cranky family members. Be creative. *You're in show business. The better you perform, the more money you make.* Do you think actors get famous by doing only *some* of the things that directors want? *Loosen up*!

Chapter Fourteen

The Information You Must Learn

Once you have a relaxed prospect whom you're controlling with mirroring, it's time to ask the crucial questions. Dr. Philip LeNoble, head of Executive Decision Systems, uses a form called the Client Needs Analysis/Customer Focus.

I've used the form successfully many times to get an accurate reading of client needs and possible level of commitment. Your station might have a similar form. The key is to develop concrete information on which to base your proposal. Some System 21 categories:

(*Total Sales*

(*Ad Budget*

(*Dollars spent-Radio, TV, Cable, Newspaper,* Yellow Pages

(*Target audience*

(*Trading Area*

(*Competition*

(*Hot and Cold Seasons*

Make sure your part of the program doesn't start until you have numbers or estimates in these areas. Your job is to provide a service; you'll be more successful with great information.

The Sandler System teaches you to gather data in a more casual manner. Sandler has you enter the initial meeting totally empty-handed. When the prospect opens up and begins to spout specific information, then say:

"Your information is important. Could I borrow a pencil and paper to take notes? I don't want to miss anything."

Sandler positions a salesperson to be the opposite of the green kid with a first-quarter package bragging about a number-one rating in males ages twelve to twenty-four, from 7 P.M. to midnight, Monday through Thursday. The Sandler person is there to assess needs. A later meeting is set for proposals. The drawback with Sandler is, without a cheat sheet, a salesperson could forget to gather information crucial to developing a successful campaign.

It might be best to save Sandler until you master mirroring, the 70/30 Rule, and probing for specific answers. Whichever system you use, this meeting is for information gathering and setting a follow-up meeting for closing the sale.

Having said that, there are exceptions. If someone is sold on the first call, by all means take the order. There'll be times when the phone interaction is so strong that it's acceptable to mention a program that fits the client perfectly.

A first-call sale may happen in TV or Cable when a bicycle shop agrees to sponsor the *Tour De France* that your network picked up. Time is crucial, so you must dial for dollars and lighten up on the niceties.

Harry Friedman, author of *Successful Retail Selling,* explains that in a busy store, it's sometimes O.K. to forget technique, cherry-pick folks who are ready to buy right now and ring them up. Those circumstances are the minority. Most times, closing new business is a struggle. That's why new business pays you more!

After you discover the information you need to make a proposal to the client, It's O.K. to talk about your station. If something the prospect says strikes a chord with one of your programs, now's the time to bring it up. A good way to do that is to say:

"You mentioned that the furniture business has a flurry of activity in October and November, then slows for a few months. Starting in September, WII FM is doing a special promotion with Drexel Heritage that might be of some interest to you. I'll research it and come back with some concrete ideas."

"Sounds interesting. How much does it cost?"

"I'm not sure yet. Let's try to meet next week, Take out your calendar. I can't go anywhere without mine."

You've made the closing appointment effortlessly without revealing that if you sell this package you win a trip to Europe. Easy isn't it?

Keep in mind that you must *never leave the prospect's office without a definite return appointment.* Do not fall for:

"Call me in the morning and we'll set something up."

That's the kiss-off of a pro. You will never reach that person again! All your hard work down the drain. Counter the indeterminate appointment with:

(Laugh) "Come on, it was almost impossible to reach you the first time and I'm running all over the place. How about next Tuesday — I'll treat you to lunch."

What you've done is provide new information. If you had just pleaded for a date, you'd be headed into "Pest-land." Instead, you sweetened the pot. Also, you find out whether your prospect likes to be wined and dined. This fact is crucial. When someone accepts an offer to break bread, he's giving in to you. Good move!

Ms. Prospect might turn down lunch but cave to setting an appointment at this juncture. If she's going to insist on no meeting, she'll stop you now. It's almost impossible to say no to the second proposal without letting the AE know the prospect is a long-term or lost project.

Once you pin down your prospect to a meeting time, pack up

and go! Your job is done for today. There might be a couple of questions you forgot to ask that are crucial to your pitch. Ask them in *Columbo* fashion as you head out the door. If you ask in that casual way, even a tough question can elicit the necessary answer.

Often the toughest fact to discover is total sales. Here are some ways around that question:

In a retail business, count the salespeople on the floor. Retailers will usually share their average sale amounts. If the average sale price is $100, each person on the floor can be expected to sell $1000–2000 per day. Count the numbers in your head and give the boss your figure. He or she will tell you if you're off base. You'll be able to interpolate from there.

Ask if they do $10 million a year. Sometimes, they'll adjust the figure for you. When they do, try to narrow more until you see the arms cross. That information will either qualify or disqualify the prospect.

Assure the prospect that the information is confidential. It's funny — merely saying the word *confidential* often works.

Almost every one of you has Internet access. Take five minutes before your meeting to research the company. Write down questions about their operation. When you ask intelligent questions, answers will start to flow more rapidly.

With qualifying sales figures in your head, set your appointment and leave. Thank Marlo on the way out. An e-mailed thank you is acceptable; it will open another window on your prospect's psyche. Nothing beats a handwritten note the next day confirming the appointment. Your prospect probably receives less than a dozen of them a year. You'll be long remembered for that touch.

What used to be the hard part of your job, cold-calling to establish trust, has been completed. Mastering *Conquering Cold-Calling Fear* techniques will turn cold calling into one of the most pleasant parts of your day. The drudgery starts now.

Chapter Fifteen

The Proposal

Now comes the part that slows down my cold calling, but gets me to the proposal. *Retail In$ights,* a monthly publication from Executive Decision Systems, Inc., provides profiles of different industries every month. Have your station subscribe to it. Then, whenever you have to do a proposal, they'll send you a one-page summary of industry standards, peak selling months, and current trends. When you return with your proposal, your prospect will have the added-value gift of new industry information.

Use the information to plan your proposal. Meet go with your sales manager after you've devised a rough plan. Going in with a "What do I do now?" attitude is an invitation to sell the current sales package.

Sales managers love to sell packages, because packages maximize available inventory, are the closest thing to a sale in media, and jack up business in first quarter. But they're often all wrong for creating a long-term client relationship.

If you believe in your heart of hearts that it's in your prospect's best interest that you push the package, go ahead and push. You invested several phone calls and a face-to-face meeting purporting to discover your prospect's needs. When you return with a canned package, you risk heading directly to Pest-land.

It's better to present special packages to existing clients who already trust you. Your manager cares about the number of packages sold, not necessarily to whom. New business packages are the exception. If new business package sales are the only item on your manager's current agenda, you might be forced to customize one to fit your new best friend's business.

When crafting a custom-made plan for your new best friend, you might as well start big. Analyze the information the prospect shared and devise an annual plan. David Bramnick, my first manager at KKSF used to say:

"It's easier to cometh down than to goeth up."

By starting with an annual plan, you do your client a favor, also. Any client who stays on a station for one year will have success. Failure in advertising is almost always guaranteed when a young salesperson sells a new client a short schedule in order to move a package demanded by management. Selling that package may save his or her job temporarily; the long-term prognosis will not be good.

Keep your presentation simple. No one has time to wade through reams of paper.

Have a personal letter on top of, or attached to, the presentation. The letter should read:

January 7, 2005

John Bentley
Discount Hardwood Furniture
18241 Pennington Drive
Detroit, MI 48221

Dear John:
It was great learning about Discount Hardwood Furniture on
Tuesday. You must be proud of all your success there.

Per your request, enclosed is a proposal designed to increase
your Drexel Heritage business while taking advantage of their
new, more generous co-op plan for 2006. Part of the program
will include sponsorship of the spring and fall Luxury Home
Shows that WII FM is proud to co-produce.

Let's work together in the coming year to form a partnership
that will cash in on the popularity of WII FM and the unique
values Discount Hardwood Furniture offers for Metro Detroiters.
Once we start the program, I'll meet with all five store managers
to fully explain what we're doing and seek their total support.

Thanks for your interest in WII FM

Best regards,

Duke Carson

Duke Carson
Account Executive, WII FM

The letter doesn't have to be long. It must have:

(*An opening paragraph never longer than three lines, preferably two.*

(*Second and third paragraphs that detail the proposal. These should be the longest — six lines maximum.*

(*A final paragraph no longer than three lines, one is best.*

(*Balance. A seasoned buyer will look at the entire letter first. If it looks unappealing, your first impression is blown.*

The prospect might never read the letter because *you are not going to hand over the proposal until your presentation is finished.* The easiest way to lose a prospect is to let her see the proposal while you're presenting. Buyers look at the last page first. Their interest can wane quickly when they see a $115,200 price tag. Your proposal must look like it's *worth a million dollars.* You haven't built the value to one dollar yet, so why let the prospect see the $115,200 tag?

The rest of the proposal should be in large type with not too much on each page. Here is where you can use Power Point to enhance the look of your proposal. If I can learn Power Point, so can you. Have someone in your office show you how to use it. In a few days you will be fine.

Mention value-added items, like Home-Show participation, first. Place a liberal dollar value on each Home Show. Place a dollar value on each promotional announcement. If the Home Show is also spending money on your station, add those dollars to your equation. When you reach the page with the thirty-second spots, add everything together like this:

HOME-SHOW PROPOSAL FOR DISCOUNT HARDWOOD FURNITURE	
Promotional announcements for Home Shows	200
Value of Home-Show announcements	$200 ea
Total Value of Home Show	$40,000
Value of Home-Show Booths	$3400
Total Value of Home-Show promotion	$43,400

When requesting a six-figure deal, it's best to feature value-added bonuses demonstrating your commitment to the client.

After adding boilerplate one-sheets about WII FM, before the last page, add the information you've discovered about how WII FM's audience buys furniture. If your station subscribes to a service like Scarborough, look up Discount Hardwood Furniture. With luck, your rating will be high. Anything over 100 in Scarborough is above average.

If you find that the store does poorly in Scarborough, try another, similar, category, like discount stores. A good showing in a related area will help. Share no information with which your competitors can come back and skewer you.

Log on to your prospect's Web site, download their logo, and incorporate it into your presentation. If you don't know how to do it, find someone at your office who does. That person, your assistant if you're lucky, can take the pieces you've assembled and turn them into something incredibly appealing. For large proposals, it's a must.

You should be ready. Most stations have much of what you need already prepared. Coordinate all parts of the proposal and add a schedule to make it look customized. A program like System 21™

(see bibliography) has a formula for how much your client can invest. Including the formula lends credibility to your proposal. If you have it, use it! The formula will keep you from proposing a six-figure budget to a prospect with $500,000 in annual sales. Businesses rarely spend more than 10 percent of sales on advertising. Exceed that figure and you *will* look and feel stupid upon presenting your proposal.

Chapter Sixteen

Switch Pitching Competitive Media

Remember: part of your success may depend on the advertiser closing out other media. A plumber will never be convinced to lower *Yellow Pages* ads, because that's the first place people look when a problem occurs. The furniture store could easily shrink *its* ad with little lost business. When was the last time you shopped for furniture in the *Yellow Pages?*

Newspaper is the fattest target. Use the George Zimmer story here. Show prospects how newspaper readers shop for bargains. Response to electronic media is more visceral, making those respondents less price-sensitive.

Use my retail advertising experience as a benchmark. Tell your prospect about a merchant who was successful using electronic media. Here's how it worked:

When I found the radio station targeted to my audience, I signed annual contracts and ran one week per month every month. People responded best when I had a great offer. Response was slowest when I used co-op advertising featuring a shoe and tagging my store at the bottom of the ad. Rather than use what the manufacturer sent me, I wrote copy myself, submitted it, and fought with the co-op people to have it approved.

Print hardly ever worked and was extremely expensive. Running co-op ads produced meager response, with one glaring exception:

City Feet conducted a semiannual survey measuring, among other things, the media our customers consumed. We found in one survey that the top station was public radio KQED FM. At the time, we were unable to advertise there, so we did the next best thing. We bought ads in their monthly program guide featured in *San Francisco Focus* magazine. Co-op dollars from Rockport, which had recently introduced a line of better-looking women's dressy casual shoes, paid for half the campaign.

The campaign worked effectively for years. We noticed middle-aged women wandering into our stores in the early afternoon as if in a trance, holding the little ad. Because we had done our research, perfectly targeting an audience, the fact that the ad wasn't totally compelling didn't kill us. It showed a product they wanted and were willing to buy at retail.

In the same survey, we found that the second most popular station was college punk rocker KFJC FM. City Feet had recently introduced Doc Marten's and Creepers to the Bay Area. From San Francisco to San Jose, punks with green spiky hair had to own a pair. KFJC was their favorite radio station. It took over a month of calling before Jennifer from KFJC finally paid a visit. When she arrived, we negotiated for City Feet to become the station's largest underwriter.

In both cases, because the station was perfectly targeted for a product the listeners wanted, price-cutting was unnecessary. Pinpoint targeting is an advantage advertisers hardly ever derive from mass-circulation newspapers.

The lesson here: Use the first meeting to determine if the business is a tight fit with what you have to sell. It's easier with TV and Cable, because there's usually something on your station that will appeal to almost everyone. Be careful. The WB catered to a large, ethnic working-class audience, while PAX TV had an older, white middle-America group. Why beat your head against the wall if the business doesn't fit comfortably into your niche?

There are one million perfectly targeted prospects who need your services. There are only five to fifteen salespeople selling the product. The law of large numbers proves there are businesses waiting for your call. Don't waste your time on marginal prospects. If you do figure a way to get them on the air, it won't work and you'll never get them back. You'll also have soured that business on your medium — maybe forever.

Remember your client's target audience when you do your due diligence. It's O.K. to return and say:

"I checked the stats and found only one area where we're a fit. It's not going to be an all-encompassing program. I think you should only advertise on our Sunday Home Decorator talk show."

Increase your credibility while making Discount Hardwood Furniture a satisfied customer.

You might not always be working at your current station. Your next sales position might be perfectly targeted for their business. Taking care of someone in a small way today often pays off tomorrow.

I have several clients who have followed me to more than one station and from radio to TV. After years of honest service, they enjoy taking my calls. When a last-minute special to sell at fire-sale rates arises, I call them first. A detailed sales pitch isn't necessary. All I have to do is present the facts. *They know I'll lie less than the average AE.*

Chapter Seventeen

The Closing Call

By now you should have your presentation ready. Let's make a deal!

Many managers tell AEs to confirm appointments. In *Conquering Cold-Calling Fear*, you've already done that with the note. Call to confirm on the day of the closing call only if it's out of town. On those occasions, contact your new best friend, Marlo the gatekeeper, and let her know you plan to arrive a few minutes early. Ask if she has any special pastry requests. Then come through with them.

Be sure to arrive on time. Nothing starts you off worse than having to apologize for tardiness. As a buyer, I often let a late salesperson wait for me as long as I had to wait for him or her. If you have a problem with punctuality, plan to arrive fifteen minutes early. Schmooze with the gatekeeper for a while upon arriving. That can only help your cause.

When caught in traffic, use your cell phone to share that dilemma with the gatekeeper, not the prospect. Have the gatekeeper inform the prospect after you hang up, so your tardiness won't be used as an excuse to cancel.

Upon meeting the prospect for the second time, be sure to remember children's and pets' names. Start with questions like:

"Has Steve started his counseling sessions yet?"

"How's Corrine the snake? Is she still lost in the house?"

The prospect needs to know that you remember. After pleasantries, review your first meeting with statements like:

"Let me review our discussion of last Tuesday. You said that your busiest season is October through Thanksgiving. Is that correct?"

Wait for an answer before proceeding.

There might be new information the prospect was unwilling to share in the first meeting. The new facts might totally change what you're prepared to present.

I once traveled to Los Angeles to pitch an annual program for Bill Simon's Western Federal Savings. There had been previous meetings, so I thought I knew what was needed. Upon arrival, the new information I gathered by probing made me rethink the program I was about to present. I put it away, returned to San Francisco for a rewrite, and returned a week later to close the largest deal in the history of Magic 61 AM.

Another reason to never surrender your presentation to the prospect until after you finish is, it allows you to try a great theatrical move. When a client hates something you've mentioned, tear out a part of the pitch the client hates before she sees it. When John says, "We don't believe in Home Shows; we'll reject any proposal with one in it," instead of trying to convince him it's a good idea, *tear it out of the presentation, ball it up, and throw it in the trash!*

You're onstage. *Act! Entertain!* Show the client you're listening. Plenty of programs will fit. If you failed to ask during the first encounter, now's the perfect time to ask:

"If you could wave a magic wand and create an advertising campaign you'd like to try but never had the opportunity, what would it be?"

You might find in the prospect's heart of hearts the idea that finally turns her on and converts you into her consultant.

A few years ago, when I posed the magic-wand question to Vicki, the owner of a small shopping center, her answer was

"An antique car show." As luck would have it, my station was capable of doing remote broadcasts using a state-of-the-art mobile studio. The center's barber, Frank, an antique car buff, was quickly recruited to send a mailer to his list soliciting entries. Before long we had developed the Millbrae Square Antique Car Show.

The show was so successful that it kept going for several years, using various radio station sponsors, long after I left KFRC. The final show featured Wolfman Jack signing autographs for four solid hours in one of his last public appearances. It remains one of my proudest experiences, all because I asked, "Has there ever been an advertising campaign you'd like to try but never had the opportunity?"

Because of my success making a longtime dream a reality, Vicki and Millbrae Square worked with me wherever I went. I was their media consultant. The more clients who see you in that role, the easier your job. You cut down on the need to continually recreate excitement. Your annual business contracts increase, and your earnings climb.

Placing the Prospect Back in State

Another reason for recreating what happened at the first meeting is to put your prospect back in the same frame of mind he was in when that meeting ended. Anthony Robbins calls it "placing the client back in state."

The prospect was excited enough with your brief outline of benefits to invite you back. Much has happened in the past week: problems with an employee, late shipments, bad weather, and a recall. All these outside factors took any thoughts of your station entirely out of the prospect's top-of-mind awareness.

You must now recreate the old atmosphere. Quickly retrace the steps that brought you back with a proposal. With every added component, ask the prospect:

"Am I remembering our conversation correctly?"

Each time your prospect agrees, you inch closer to a final yes, placing your services back into the prospect's top-of-mind awareness. Hold off your pitch until the client is back in state. A client still fixated on the aforementioned annoyances is not ready to hear your story.

Expert Kills the Deal

You might see a surprise player attend the second meeting. Possibly, the person you thought was the ultimate decision-maker was actually someone with only the power to say no. The big boss is brought in only when an underling thinks his or her intercession is warranted.

When this happens, never say:

"But I thought you made all the decisions here."

It's important to make sure you understand the new person's power position. A great way to put it is:

"Glad you could join us. It's crucial that everyone in a position of authority share in important decisions. Can you fill me in on what some of your duties are at Discount Hardwood?"

In the shoe business, we called it *expert kills the deal*. The wife came in, tried on shoes, liked them, and was ready to buy. The husband joined her after battling for a parking space, and trashed her pick.

As soon as we saw this coming, we addressed the husband. Since he was obviously an *expert*, we asked him to help us out.

"A new style of men's shoes just arrived, and we haven't had time to check them out yet. Would you (the acknowledged expert on all topics) try on a pair and let us know how they fit?

Sound familiar? "Would you help us out?" Nearly everyone wants to appear helpful. Once his shoes were off he was neutralized, and we could proceed to close the sale with his wife. His opinion of the shoes he was trying on was of no importance to us. We had succeeded in placing him in sync with his wife and the shoe-store staff. Now all we had to do was worry about finding a fit for his wife.

The expert can kill you in any closing meeting. Remember: this meeting was *not* the new participant's idea. There might be competition between your guy and the expert. Win the expert over right away, or start hearing a chorus of increasingly tough questions. Those questions will be the cue for your original prospect to lose interest.

You must win the expert over the same way you did the prospect. Start by asking:

"I asked John how he got started at Discount. How did you end up here, Justin?"

Getting to a personal level with Justin is like getting the husband to take off his shoes. Failure to get the expert's figurative shoes off means you face a tougher battle.

A problem I see in many salespeople is the lack of courage to press on with a workable technique, like asking for a life history. They fear angering a blustery prospect and being thrown out of the meeting. If that's the worst thing that happens, you'll survive the experience and add a great cocktail party story to your repertoire.

When a prospect gets angry and tells you to leave before you've finished the session, do the following:

Let him finish his tirade.

When he finishes, do nothing, say nothing, and silently count to ten.

What will usually happen then is a quick apology for his being so loutish.

If that doesn't happen, say:

"O.K., now that you've gotten that off your chest, let's get down to business."

I know it's hard to keep your cool under these conditions, but if you do, your respect level will skyrocket and a new friendship will be born.

Bullies hate having their bluff called. Remember when you were a kid and someone finally stood up to the playground bully? Was that a great feeling?

When I was starting out, I tried to sell encyclopedias door to door in Los Angeles. The head of the *Encyclopedia Britannica* office was a grizzled, thrice-divorced, hard-drinking, overweight, lovable rogue named Al Winfield.

Al took me on four sales presentations and closed all four. The toughest was at the upscale house of a Swedish engineer, his wife and two kids. About two minutes into Al's spiel, the Swede went nuts on Winfield. He was pacing back and forth, berating Al as a lying thief who was selling a product he didn't need at an incredibly inflated price. The fact that everything the guy said was right on didn't bother Winfield a bit.

I started to get up and bolt when Al pushed me back. He sat there calmly until the Swede finished. I watched in amazement as the guy apologized to both his wife and us before Winfield went on to sell him the least expensive set of books and throw in the free bookcase, atlas, and dictionary.

Winfield's patience, born of perfect technique, salvaged an apparently impossible situation. The histrionics earned the best possible deal for the Swede. Win-win!

That was my first experience in the *courage* it takes to be a successful new-business developer. There have been hundreds more. Keep in mind that many times a prospect is gruff because he or she knows that once you penetrate the tough façade, he or she is an easy mark. Some of my favorite clients had reputations for chewing up and spitting out AEs regularly.

I mention all these pitfalls on your way to a successful relationship so you'll be prepared when they arise. Anyone can close easy deals; you're on your way to being able to close sales that previous AEs at your station have lost. Each time that happens, your boss will remember. A good sales manager will reward you for tough sales — you're making her look good while increasing year-end bonuses for new business.

Back to the meeting. Once you've worked Justin back into your corner, it's time to finish reviewing the parameters you were given to develop your proposal. Make sure all parties agree on the size of their business, the budget, and the times of the year best suited to advertising. If you're all still in sync, you can bring out the proposal.

Never hand the proposal to the prospect. Take it out and use it as your guide to the presentation. If the client asks to see it, let him know you'll leave a copy when you finish. The best presentations take five to ten minutes. You've used the previous twenty-five minutes putting the client in the perfect frame of mind.

If the prospect believes in you, even an average pitch will succeed in closing the sale. When you fail to establish a relationship, a perfect presentation will fall on deaf ears. Have you ever felt that you were presenting to a totally unresponsive prospect? The relationship wasn't fully developed. You were doomed.

Your presentation should dwell on benefits. Start with:

"Wouldn't it be great if Discount Hardwood Furniture were at the top of homeowner's minds when they think of wood furniture? The quickest way to do that is through consistency."

Then you can add:

"Remember the story of George Zimmer's success with The Men's Wearhouse?"

You're laying the groundwork for an annual commitment. It's time to add that research through System 21™ shows that after three months, the target audience starts to know you. After six months, they know about you and your business. After a year, your business is top of mind to your station's 400,000 listeners/viewers.

Here, you must caution the prospect that most new advertisers will realize the full effect of their ad campaign only after a full year. The first three months are laying groundwork; there may be little measurable response. Usually the fourth month starts to show movement. It builds from there. After a year, there should be marked improvement in sales if other elements of the campaign are working.

Facts and figures are great, but must be accompanied by benefits. When you give numbers:

"This program gives you over 500 commercials."

You must add:

"That means your message will reach 400,000 listeners an average of twenty-eight times each. With that kind of coverage, you're well on your way to building a household name."

If the prospect responds:

"How do I know those people will buy my furniture?"

You must return to your previous week's discussion.

"Remember we discovered that WII FM listeners showed up well on the last Scarborough Report as shoppers for hardwood furniture?"

"Yes, I do."

Add:

"There are no guarantees in advertising. All we can do is make an educated guess. Doesn't it make sense that if our audience is predisposed to buying your products, and is exposed to your message at least 776 times next year, there's a good probability that, if your offers are compelling, they'll give you a try?"

"That does make sense. But it's so much money!"

Now remind John of the earlier statement he made about the size of Discount Hardwood Furniture and his goals for next year. Present your new information by saying:

"You *are* committed to raising sales 10 percent next year aren't you?"

"Well... sure... but — "

"Here's how we're going to do it."

System 21 has a formula for figuring this out. For those who haven't been exposed to that system, do the following:

CURRENT SALES	
$700,000	Ad Budget
$11,000,000	Projected next year sales
$770,000	Budget
$350,000	Current Newspaper
$300,000	Projected next year
$115,200	WII-FM Plan
$5,000	Next year's ad budget surplus
Total announcements	776
Average price per announcement	$148

You're in control because you remember that Discount had sales of $10 million last year and a budget of 7 percent for advertising. They spent the $700,000, but might be willing to cut back on newspaper advertising. They want to grow the business 10 percent next year, so they'll have an additional $70,000 to spend. With the $70,000 and a 10 percent cut in their newspaper budget, which was determined to be $350,000, there will be money to spare. In fact, the ad percentages will be slightly lower.

In retail sales training, Harry Friedman taught us to give the customer only two benefits when selling a pair of shoes. We might say:

"This shoe has a rubber sole, making it more comfortable for you to stand all day. Also, it's made of Italian leather, so the upper will look presentable when you meet the public."

Then ask for the sale. If that was enough, the sale is closed. If the customer is still not convinced, mention another benefit, like:

"The shoes can be resoled, saving you money on buying another pair." Then try to close again. You might have to do this three times before making the sale. The point is, *never spill all the benefits at once.*

Save something for an emergency. If the client has a question, you'd best have an answer hiding in your back pocket. Begging won't earn you the respect necessary for a long-term relationship, and probably won't be enough to save the sale, anyway. Why bother?

You've just given John a dollars-and-cents reason why WII FM is a smart buy. It's based on the WII FM philosophy espoused by Paul Karasik, founder of ASLA:

What's In It for Me, WII FM?

What's in it for John of Discount Hardwood Furniture is higher sales on a slightly lower percentage of advertising. If his sales figures come in on budget, he'll make additional profit next year. That kind of argument sells!

While letting the dollars-and-cents argument sink in, remind John:

"I understand your concern. You're spending your own hard-earned dollars. That's where I come in. I want you as a permanent part of my business. It's difficult to continually find new clients. I'm lazy that way. I don't want to put folks on the air for a few weeks and then start again a short while later with someone brand-new.

My goal is to have fewer, stronger clients. The only way to do that is to make money for people like you. If your campaign falters, I will personally change whatever is necessary to try to make it work. Let me share what I did with Apple Computer.

Apple Computer Business Systems was an Apple unit that ran seminars for business owners interested in possibly using Apple computers for their office applications.

At the time, the Apple unit didn't have a memorable telephone number. I suggested that, since they were relying on phone response, they should find a more catchy number. Not convinced, they started the program with the old number. Even though my station, KKSF, had extremely high ratings for both computer users and Apple Computer lovers, response was tepid.

"I finally convinced the client to find a catchier number. They came up with 1-800-5-APPLE-9. The first time we tried it, response doubled. Apple continued as a client for years."

Use the story. If you feel uncomfortable saying *you* did it, say a friend of yours had the experience.

I'll bet you've had similar experiences, where *you* went the extra mile to save a deal and wound up with a long-term client. Here's the time to use that story. Let the prospect know you've worked overtime before. With the story, future promises will be more believable.

Showmanship!

The proposal I outlined earlier needs to be explained, so John understands that your station is offering much more than he is buying. When you go through the list, pump up the value of the Home Shows as an added sales floor that might bring in enough business to pay for a good portion of the ad budget. Home Shows are venues to test new products for immediate customer feedback. Ask:

"What if someone who has never heard of your store comes by your booth at the show and decides to spend $25,000 to furnish a new home? That's not an unreasonable assumption. People buy $25,000 roofs, expensive heating systems, and $100,000 room additions. Why not your furniture?

"What if you picked up ten new customers who each spend $10,000 in your stores next year? You've paid for the campaign. The rest is gravy."

Give everything value. By the time you're through, your package should be worth $1 million for an investment of around $100,000. What a *bargain*! I'm getting excited *writing* about the promotion.

When you finish, stop and say nothing. See what kind of response you receive. Check the body language while you're giving the pitch. Are they still with you physically? If they are and say nothing, assume they agree to the sale.

Many sales books teach that the first person to talk loses. We're not trying to beat anybody. We want this to be the start of a great relationship. We've offered a great deal, lots of value added, and a reason to buy based on a potential business increase that will actually lower the percentage of John's ad budget to total sales.

Continue looking for closing signals. If he says:

"I can't do this right now."

Answer:

"When can you start?"

If he says:

"Not for four months."

You say:

"Perfect. That will give us extra time to have everything in place for you. Would June or July be better?"

You have a new client. Congratulations!

If he's still wavering, say:

"The schedule calls for two weeks per month of commercials. Would you like to do two weeks on, two weeks off, or every other week?"

That statement usually works well. It offers a choice of two options, each closing the sale.

John might reply:

"I think every other week would be better, but I'm still not sure. What about production? That's usually so expensive."

You step in and answer:

"If I found a way to give you free production, would that be enough to get started today?"

"Well...yes."

"Can I use your phone?"

Call the station and ask for the production department. Radio production is usually free, unless outside talent is brought in. Make a point of asking the production director (whom I will talk about in later chapters) if he can give John from Discount Hardwood free production. When you hang up the phone, stick out your hand to shake on the deal. Let John know you negotiated the free production for him.

Production in TV and Cable is a more difficult proposition. Often, medium-sized advertisers refrain from TV over fear of poor production values. We've all seen cheesy local commercials on air. Many businesses shudder to think their precious business will be degraded in such a fashion.

Your job is to assure John of your production crew's experience and state-of-the-art equipment. Assure John that no spot will air unless he gives final approval. This is a good time to start discussing what his vision of the spot should be. Invite John to the editing studio.

If you know your station *must* charge for production, either build it into the cost of the spots, or explain the vast difference between doing the spot at the station or at an agency. The agency might charge ten times as much the station — the $1500 John will spend with you is peanuts compared with an agency's fee.

Now is a good time to ask John if he'd like to be featured in the spot. Business owners have big egos, or they'd be unsuccessful. It's unseemly for them to come right out and ask to be in the spot. You're the one who must broach the subject.

Contrary to popular belief, George Zimmer had to be pushed, kicking and screaming, to do the Men's Wearhouse spots. When the agency approached him he thought they were nuts. He was not good looking, had a funny way of talking, and was a terrible actor. If you remember, his first spots years ago were horrible.

Zimmer had the credibility of the storeowner. If he said, "I guarantee it," people believed him. Here was a regular guy selling at a discount to regular people. They could relate to him more closely than to a handsome actor with a perfect physique.

The same thing happened to me at City Feet. I was running a successful radio campaign on KPEN FM, designed by Peter B. Collins. Peter received extra payment for each commercial he voiced. One day, my AE, Michael Jacoby, proposed that I voice the spots myself, save the talent fee, and establish a personality for the store.

I didn't have to be asked more than once. My dream was to be on the radio. Why not pay my way on and see what happened? If it killed business, I was prepared to try Peter B. again.

I was a minor hit in the spots. The radio campaign was a huge success. Business improved. When customers entered one of the stores and recognized my voice, it was a sure sale. Being on the radio gave me a selling advantage. Customers were ever so slightly in awe.

After four successful years, the station was sold. Many people came into the store and asked if there was something I could do to keep the new owner from changing the Jazz-Fusion format. I did meet with the man, but was unable to convince him to stop the foolish change to easy listening. The new format flopped.

If you can convince your prospect to be in the commercial, boom! The deal is closed. Use your head. Refrain from asking owners with disfigurements or speech impediments to do their own spots. You'll just look stupid making what they know is an insincere suggestion. Owner-spokespersons can be extremely effective. Proposing they try it is an effective close.

I bring up different closing techniques for problem prospects. If you did your mirroring both on the phone and in person, much of what I recently mentioned might not be necessary. Remember the 70/30 Rule. When you came back to that closing meeting, did you bring the prospect back to the charmed state of mind and get him talking about his business? Did you create an atmosphere of trust and warmth? If you succeeded, you should have fewer problems with your proposal.

Let's say you've done everything right, but the client is simply not ready. As a consultant, pushing hard for a close might border on improper behavior. Before you give up for the day, set another meeting. Remember: *never leave without a token of success.* At the next meeting, be prepared to answer more of the prospect's questions.

You can leave the proposal if the client likes it and has legitimate reasons for stalling. Let's say she plans a three-week vacation. You should already know where she's going and why. I promise you, when she returns, she will have totally forgotten your pitch. Maybe you should try:

"It's going to be tough returning from Tahiti to face the Home-Show pitch. Why don't we decide today to move forward, and we can firm up the details when you return. Meanwhile, I'll reserve a space in both shows and set aside enough inventory to handle your needs."

What if you've done everything right, are sure you have the prospect in your sights, go for the close, and hear:

"I love the plan and want to do it. All that's left now is clearing it by [pick one] the board of directors, the owner, my husband, my partner."

Your response must be:

"Great! When can we meet them?"

Do not let the prospect off the hook until you have a chance to meet with the ultimate decision-maker. If the prospect says that's impossible, say:

"You know more about your business than I do, John. I wouldn't attempt to try to sell an important client of yours a $20,000 bedroom set.

"Of course not."

"It's the same with you trying to sell radio advertising. You probably wouldn't be as effective as I would. That's why it's crucial I accompany you to the presentation."

That pitch has a 50-50 chance of success.

You are about to give over the explanation of your beloved proposal to someone who can hardly understand it himself. Scary! Ask if you can at least speak to the actual decision-maker *on the phone.* Maybe that tactic will give you the chance for a face-to-face with him or her.

If the answer is still no, let your new friend know that he or she will need to fully understand the pitch before presenting it to "the boss." Your chances of an early sale have diminished 80 percent. If you're unable to convince the prospect to let you near the boss, your hopes ride on an amateur selling your package. I don't envy you.

When you know the close will not come today, make another appointment and leave gracefully. Most decent-sized sales aren't closed on the first try. The average is five meetings. It might take you ten meetings to close the first deal. Each time you meet, a closer relationship is forged.

If your favorite close isn't mentioned here, don't worry. When the relationship is solid, business closes itself at a high rate. Tricks are less important.

What Are Some of the Closes You Have Used Successfully?

Take five minutes to make a list of closes that have worked for you. E-mail your best to coldcall-nofear.com. Each close used in the next edition of *Conquering Cold-Calling Fear* will be noted and rewarded.

Chapter Eighteen

Following Up

Your success at arranging an appointment to pitch your station doesn't mean the prospect is in any way ready to change her current advertising mix. Often, prospects have annual print or electronic contracts that must be honored. If that's the case, learn the firm end dates for the contracts before you leave. Note the information in your contact file, and make a call at least ninety days before end dates to avoid the prospect's using the same excuse a second time.

Your station needs *Yellow Pages* closing dates for all books in your prospect's trading area. Call the *Yellow Pages* to secure those dates. Return before the close date to switch a business that needs to wean itself of its *Yellow Pages* burden.

With e-commerce such a strong presence, there's less need for the huge outlays businesses have been forced to make with the phone company. Your prospect might not be ready for e-listings. She knows the *Yellow Pages* heyday is over. You need to be there to pick up the pieces.

One of the first things I did after finding the perfect radio station for my shoe stores was cut *Yellow Pages* ad costs. When City Feet had a large *Yellow Pages* presence, callers price-checked our most popular shoes. There were always competitors selling for a dollar less. Those *Yellow Pages* shoppers never came in the store.

Worse yet, they received the impression that City Feet was over-priced on everything, causing us to *lose* business. Once I dropped the size of the ad and placed the dollars on radio, my customer base became less price-sensitive.

Now that you know the important dates, use your contact file to keep in touch with prospects. They'll need you in the future. Discard only the prospects who fail to qualify due to low sales volume, lack of capital, or poor target audience. Viable prospects need contacting when something new and better suited to their needs presents itself.

One of the benefits I provide for everyone on my list is a *periodic newsletter.* If you're creative, make it resemble a newspaper filled with station news and special promotions. Include a call to action for a station prize at the bottom. I usually have a 5 percent return rate. I've closed some sales with the newsletter. A newsletter is useful for contacting folks you don't have time to call regularly. The next time you call, they'll swear they talked to you recently — when it was actually the newsletter.

Chapter Nineteen

After the Close

When the prospect says yes, he becomes a client. Congratulations! Go ahead; pat yourself on the back. *Once he says yes, do not say another word about your station.* His decision is based on the information you have selectively provided. Why take the chance of saying something that will change his mind? There could be a DJ on your station he dislikes. Perhaps your station carries "The Jerry Springer Show," and he believes Jerry is in bad taste. So shut up and write. Before you leave, ask this important question:

"What was it that made you choose WII FM?"

Let your new client give you rational reasons for a decision that was partly emotional.

The value of recounting the reasons for the buy is to keep buying benefits top of mind and prevent buyer's remorse. When you leave, John will call his assistant into the room and offer a rational explanation for the decision. Each time he repeats those reasons, they become more like a mantra, further solidifying his decision.

Without elucidating concrete reasons for the buy, John might become confused and uncertain as to his motives. He might say:

"That Julie is quite a salesperson, but I'm not sure we need radio at this time."

Don't take that chance. Upon leaving, write down John's reasons for buying. If buyer's remorse becomes an issue, you can nip it with the "facts" John mentioned.

Most radio/TV/Cable deals are not by written contract. Clients who want to cancel simply give a standard two-weeks' notice. To solidify your arrangement, give your client a credit application to sign. Regardless of whether the client is ultimately creditworthy, signing the credit app is like signing a contract. The way I put it is:

"In order to set the wheels in motion, we ask that you sign this credit application. How's your credit, by the way?"

Look right in his eyes when you ask that question.

I know you finished the positive experience of closing the sale. Now you turn into the mean credit manager. Clients need to know as soon as possible that you *will* collect your money. Your new client's reaction is telling.

Many firms have a credit app on their letterhead ready to go, and merely hand it to you. If your new client takes a deep breath before answering, you know there will be problems. The moment you notice such a reaction, say:

"The credit app is for identification only. We operate on a C.O.D. basis for the first few sales until we establish a payment pattern."

Now you're thinking fast by observing body language. Signing the credit app seals the deal. Leave the building. There'll be time to celebrate when you return to the station. With a new client, you have much to do before he goes on the air.

Internal Selling — Sometimes the Hardest Part

You've made the sale. Now you have to face your sales manager with the ugly details. After a little experience, you generally know how much wiggle room is available with each deal. It's rare that a client accepts your first offer. Financial negotiations often start *after* you've convinced the prospect that your station, package, and timing are perfectly matched to his or her business.

Here's a rule that will keep you on an even footing when negotiating with a new client"

Always get when you give!

When John asks me to round off the $115,200 package to $100,000,
I say:

"Sure I'll be glad to lower the price. What are you willing to
give up for the $15,200? I can lower the amount of paid or promo
spots. We could stretch the time periods on the paid spots from
Drive Time to 5 A.M.–8 P.M. Which would you prefer?"

By appearing reasonable but offering little, you're doing another type of fogging. In the end, your LSM can probably be accept
your giving away $15,000 in promo spots that don't affect your
bottom line as much as paid. John needs to feel that you're going
the extra mile for him. If he counters that he absolutely can't go
into a six-figure contract, lower the deal to $99,000, or tell him
you'll write it up in two separate contracts if necessary.

The key issue is, when you finally give the concession, be sure
it seals the deal. Say:

"I can't go back to my manager with preliminary negotiations.
If I agree to give you over $15,000 in free advertising, do we have
a deal?"

You've placed John in the perfect position. At this point, you'll
almost always make the deal, unless John says he can't guarantee anything yet. Then you know you have more work ahead.
Patience.

Save preliminary deals from your manager unless you're so far
apart that the deal needs to be totally restructured. He or she will
think you aren't a good closer and don't understand the product
enough to convince a prospect that the benefits are worth far
more than the asking price.

When you have to cut the price drastically to make a deal, be sure
you write up the sale on your order form and then slip it into
your computer-generated manager's box or enter it into your system

right away. *Then* go to the manager and explain why you had to pull your pants down so far to make the deal. *It's always better to say you're sorry than to ask permission.*

One of the reasons this book is called *Conquering Cold-Calling Fear Before and After the Sale* is that, when you become comfortable calling strangers, you also learn how to handle internal station battles. Comfort in the most unpleasant sales task increases confidence elsewhere.

Your increased confidence will lead to a higher average unit rate on your contracts, because your strengthened relation ship with clients will make it easier for you to maintain rate integrity. You will become their consultant. People pay more for consultants than for salespeople. As your confidence grows, you'll spend less time in the manager's office begging for a lower client rate. With improved technique, requests for lower rates to close deals will become rare. When they're necessary, your manager will accept them without charging you psychic points.

Taking Care of Support Staff

Another reason to write up the sale today is to eliminate mistakes. I can't stress this enough. Track the sale all the way to contract state. Television AEs often have assistants write up orders. Place every order given to an assistant in an electronic or written tickler file. Double-check the next day to make sure the contract was entered.

One reason for continual checking:

The more sales you have, the more work you create for support staff. You make more money with more sales; their pay stays the same. It's crucial to train assistants to enter contracts accurately and quickly. Train in the most pleasant manner possible. Consider your assistant a person who needs and merits praise regularly. The more work you pile on, the more flowers, candy, and lunches you need to provide.

Soon after I opened my first shoe store we had a great Saturday. At the end of the day I was ecstatic. I enthused to salesperson Elizabeth Morgan what a great day it was. She turned to me and sneered:

"For you, maybe. We all just worked harder for the same money."

I soon instituted a commission sales system, so everyone would work toward the same goal.

Managers should institute a group reward system to keep everyone working in the same direction all the time. (It hasn't existed at any radio or TV station where I worked.) Try it with your support staff and see how productivity grows.

Even with a reward system in place, your assistant will generally not last more than a year. Someone new will have to be trained. Mistakes occur during training time. Please keep a file of every order. Nothing looks more ridiculous than admitting to a client that his schedule, which you worked so hard placing, never ran.

You should emphasize to your assistant the importance of entering orders properly. Be firm, consistent, and fair when you stress the point. I learned the hard way always to maintain a double-checking system when someone else writes my orders.

Half of a major department store's March orders were never entered one year because I hired a friend to help out during a temporary emergency. She misplaced the orders and I failed to double-check. Fortunately for me, my relationship was so solid with the buyer that she continued doing business with my network.

Traffic Department Pitfalls

Think your assistant is a big problem? Check out the traffic department! Some traffic directors (TDs) think the station revolves around their jobs. Where they place your spots can mean the difference between a happy new client and a new former one. Poor placement of new business has killed deals. TDs must always be treated with the utmost respect.

Thou shalt never engage in a pitched battle with the traffic director, unless thou planneth on leaving the area soon. I've known traffic directors who ranged from total professionals, who'd bend over backwards to make sure your orders were entered correctly, to greed-mongers who asked for concert tickets every week.

Strong TD relations are especially important in TV, where there are infinitely more chances for error than in radio. Try to be the station's best in paperwork submitted to traffic. It's bad enough that you're writing the most business; when those orders are consistently a mess, you make TDs work overtime..

Often, the traffic director's status is equal to that of the local sales manager (LSM). The LSM is trying to force as many spots into prime areas as you are. He or she can't afford to piss off the TD either. At a busy TV station the two department heads are constantly in touch. Take the few extra seconds to double-check what you submit, so you become known as the salesperson with the best paperwork.

Institute a *baksheesh* plan with the TD by learning his or her likes and dislikes. Operate as you've been taught to with gatekeepers. You will need favors. Build up a reserve of goodwill by taking care of someone who has the power to take care of you.

Your manager will force you any times to sell broader day-parts than the client prefers. Close the deal by promising to ride herd on spot placement. Then try for prime-location spots at lower rates. Follow-up by going, hat in hand, to traffic, and beg for better placement.

A smart TD will give new clients the best possible rotation to help an AE keep the client on the air. Ask for special placement only when absolutely necessary. Keep the TD on your team by picking the right spots to beg, and your new business clients will have an easier road to success. AEs who beg all the time soon find their pleas falling on deaf ears, unless the TM is totally corrupt, and gift giving continually escalates.

Chapter Twenty

Producing Your Commercial

Your schedule is properly entered and placed. Now you have to produce a spot that will sell. The first rule of constructing a winning spot: *Institutional spots don't work!*

As you closed the sale, you might have discussed how John wanted his store presented. When he shared the information that he already had a spot, or series of spots, you should have asked to review them. Sometimes they're great, and all you need to do is ask a competing station for copies.

If the creative isn't up to what you consider your station's standards, either dated, poor quality, bad message or not compelling, don't let your disgust show on your face. Merely say:

"Nice spots. How did they do?"

Wait for John to tell *you* he hates the spots. Never be the one to volunteer such information. Doing so says, in effect:

"How could you be so dumb as to allow this great store to be depicted in such a small-market manner?"

Good way to blow a sale that was already closed.

Many times, the client will be disgusted with what went on before and want to upgrade. If he or she states the case for change and asks again for your opinion, critique tactfully. If the spot was too institutional, ask:

"What was your goal with this spot? Did you achieve it?"

John might say he wanted to show the depth of Discount Hard-wood Furniture's inventory. The campaign didn't generate additional foot traffic, so John will be open to something new.

That's when I go into the retail experience I mentioned earlier: *Price and item bring people into stores;* upon arrival, they'll see the incredible inventory for themselves.

I once tried a heavy-metal station KSJO for City Feet. I put a style of shoe I thought appropriate on sale for $17, about one-third the regular price — an irresistible offer. The huge discount was necessary to draw customers listening to a new station.

My rule of thumb for radio was always twenty-four spots to achieve a three frequency and reach the target audience properly.

We ran the spots. Many people came in. Their response was:

"Seventeen dollars — are you *crazy?* I would never pay that much for shoes!"

O.K., it was a long time ago. The point is that the test worked. I drove people into my stores with a great offer. The fact that they were the wrong people was O.K. with me. I gained valuable market research for a one-week investment. When the AE called the following week to learn the results of the test, I thanked him for his help and explained the findings. He had no comeback. I never was tempted to use that station again.

If I had run a co-op ad campaign, it might have taken me two months and eight times the investment to get my results. Had the AE been more skilled, he wouldn't have allowed me to do the test. For one short-term hit, he ruined his station forever with a client who believed in his medium.

I bring up the KSJO incident to emphasize the power of price/item advertising. Explain to John that we want the campaign to work at least as much as he does. If he's going to be on for twelve consecutive months, let's plan a campaign featuring season-appropriate furniture with a special offer.

January	Rocking Chairs	Were $199	Now $129
February	Bedroom Sets	$1500	Now $999
March	Home-Show Specials		
April	Patio Sets	$650	Now $399
May	Play Structures	$1750	Now $1299
June	Adirondack Chairs	$575	Now $369
July	Summer Clearance	All Summer merchandise 40% off	
August	Home-Show Specials		
September	Maple Dining Sets	Were $2750	Now $1999
October	Pre-Holiday Living Room Sale –Save Hundreds!		
November	Turkey Day Specials		
December	End-of-Year Clearance		

Go through the year with John. Maybe there's a month with so little business that John wants to skip advertising. Take those dollars and double up in the hot months. Dr. Philip LeNoble uses the phrase:

"Shoot the ducks while they're flying."

Encourage John to spend in the appropriate months, and have an offer each time.

You are John's media consultant. Be as strong here as in closing the sale. The longer John takes to see results, the more nervous you both become. Convince him to use compelling copy and double your chance of success.

Making Co-op Dollars Work Harder for Your Client

You can circumvent John's fear of losing co-op ad dollars selling merchandise at a discount by pounding on his manufacturers' co-op ad departments. Volunteer to talk to them.

I worked co-op departments by writing copy *mentioning* the advertiser a proper number of times in radio, and *showing* them enough on TV. I then called the co-op ad director, and used cold-calling techniques described earlier to make my case. Sometimes the spots were O.K. as written; other times, we had to make changes. Much depended upon my relationship with the co-op director.

It takes a bit of work on John's part. Let him call. You rewrite. Soon, you're a full-fledged consultant. You achieved co-op on sale items John would never have dreamed of requesting. Businesses face a constant battle collecting rightfully earned co-op dollars. Anyone showing them the way to more dollars is a hero.

Now that the co-op dollars are flowing, it's time to produce the spot. Radio spots are relatively easy to produce, and are usually done free for the client. If your station has the luxury of a staff copywriter, sit down with copy points and any developed ideas, to see if you can create a campaign that sells. Keep in mind that unless the copywriter has sales experience, you run the risk of a beautifully crafted spot that sells nothing.

My all-time favorite copywriter is Bryan Rhea. He started working with me at nineteen years old on some memorable City Feet ads. We hooked up again at Magic 61, where he wrote hard-selling ads that enabled new radio advertisers to gain quick acceptance. His booming voice is perfect for fast-moving items or going-out-of-business sales. The key factor is his ability to home in on the words that make people enter a store or pick up the phone.

Don't worry if you find yourself in a situation where *you* must do the copy. Right now you might be thinking, *I don't know how to write a commercial!* Part of your job is at least to know a bad one when you see it. Why not ask your client to write something and have you edit it? Coming up with an idea is often the hardest part. Editing is easier. There's probably some senior AE or LSM on the staff who'll be willing to proof the spot.

Don't be afraid to ask the production people. They think they know it all, anyway. Here's their chance to prove it.

Humor is hard. Try it only if you're already good at writing humor. Otherwise, it will fall flat or not be understood. Wait until you're comfortable with the client and the subject matter before trying funny stuff.

Here are some suggestions for radio:

(*Mention the advertiser at least four times in sixty seconds on radio.*

(*If the advertiser has a great phone number and wants people to call, feature it prominently. One good way is to say:*
"Get a pencil and write down the number we'll mention at the end of this message."

(*Make sure there's a call to action, like:*
"Call today," or "Limited quantities," or "Sale ends February fifth."

(*Be generous, especially with a new advertiser.*

New listeners need more than 15 percent off sales. That's not enough. Try:
"Sofas...Were $899, now $499."

Many people can't figure percentages. Unless it's half off, you lose some folks. Better to quote a "was/now" scenario similar to that one on the sofas.

With few total words to use, try not to say the same words in consecutive sentences, other than to make a point like:
"2003 Cadillacs are priced not at thirty-nine thousand, not at

thirty-*six* thousand, not even at thirty-*four* thousand. This week at Southfield Cadillac, all 2003 Cadillacs are at the unbelievably low price of *twenty-nine thousand nine hundred and ninety dollars!* At these prices, we'll sell out fast, so *hurry* to Southfield Cadillac, 12345 Telegraph Avenue at Eleven-Mile road. Southfield Cadillac — Cadillacs at Chevy prices!"

You're in a creative business. This is the fun part. Enjoy it. Let your creative juices flow.

If your new client is part of a station promotion, be sure it's a fit. A good example is giving away free movie passes at a video store. When you do, be sure to say, "Limited to stock on hand." That prevents mooches from coming in and demanding tickets after the promotion ends.

When the owner will be the spokesperson, be sure he or she practices the lines before going on mike. Offer a script with the emphasized words underlined. If the spokesperson has trouble with a word or phrase, find a new one to better fit his or her speech patterns. Always have a glass of water ready. Cotton-mouth is the norm.

Most DJs are assigned production time. You might wind up working with one who'd rather be playing golf. Make life easier by coming prepared to the session. Be sure the DJ is clear on the concept of what you're attempting.

You have to take charge. Some DJs are satisfied with mediocrity, especially those who are legends in their own minds. Approve their work only when your client is satisfied. Point out anything that's not perfect in a pleasant manner. Make them play the spot again, so they'll notice what needs changing.

Have the client in the studio with you to sign off on the finished product. During production, there can never be enough ears in radio or eyes in TV. Client participation is crucial for pronunciation of trade-sensitive words, like the names of the cities where the stores are located. Empower your client to speak up until he or she is satisfied. It's better for your relationship with the production department that the client asks for more takes.

Concord is a city near San Francisco. We can always tell when an out-of-towner has voiced a commercial for a store there, because they pronounce it *Con-cord* instead of the local pronunciation, *Con-kerd*.

You want your client involved, but not to the point of doing something you know will ruin the spot. Stand up and tell him when he's wrong. A good way to do this is to remind him that if this campaign fails, he'll blame you. He needs to trust your years of experience in making spots that sell.

Not long ago, a New-Age company seeking an audience of women aged thirty-five to sixty-four agreed to a rather large TV commitment with a station I represented. They sought subscribers for the launch of a magazine. The CEO had her in-house publicity manager write the script. Fine with me — I had a hard time grasping their concept and, until then, was unable to write anything coherent.

They arrived at the session with a convoluted image piece. I asked Sunny, the CEO, where was the call to action. She replied that the spot was an image enhancer. Trouble was brewing. I said:

"Excuse me, Sunny, but this spot needs a grabber, or no one will know what you want them to do."

Her entourage consisted of several attractive women who were unwilling or afraid to tell Sunny that the empress had no clothes.

"Don't worry, we're taking full responsibility for the spot. It's part of our image campaign."

I was powerless to prevent the upcoming disaster. Of course, the spots were horrible. Nobody responded. My station was blamed. The contract was not renewed. An AE friend from my previous station heard the monstrosity and quickly signed up Sunny for a six-figure jingle package.

The station, KOFY TV, had contracted with a jingle creator to produce high-quality product for small advertisers in exchange for six-figure contracts. They developed a much better campaign. It was going great until Sunny's mother was arrested for having embezzled money from San Francisco State University to finance this bizarre project. The jingle station never got paid. Sunny and her mother await trial.

You see, most small advertisers are spending their own money. When they trust your expertise, they want you to have as much input as possible. They're used to trusting experts. When one of them is totally off-the-wall, ask whether they have the money for the campaign. Business owners rarely spend gobs of money irrationally.

You're in the studio and the DJ is terrible. Try not to insult him. Make a note to stay away from that talent in the future. Keep on him until something is produced. Then tell your production director that the client prefers someone else. There's no need to hurt feelings when you can avoid it. Don't allow inferior product on the air. Merely re-record with another voice. Your reputation is at stake — as is the client's money.

If you're at a station where the DJs are major personalities, you can suggest that a particular DJ do the spots in the form of a testimonial. Testimonials sell better, and when they're done by famous personalities, the chance of success skyrockets.

Your DJs have to do spots. You can request a particular DJ on a permanent basis, or ask him or her to use the term *we* instead of *they* when describing the business. You'll have to pay for that little change of wording. If it's important to the client, work out a simple payment plan — usually in the hundreds, rather than thousands, per spot. If Howard Stern cuts your spot, then thousands are involved.

DJs make surprisingly little unless they're one of the top five talents in the market. Any token of appreciation will be to your benefit. Over the years, DJs seem to be the one easygoing part of a station. You'd think they might be the prima donnas, but they have too much fun being DJs to worry about station politics.

Make sure the client is satisfied with the final product. If, for some reason, the client is unable to attend the session, never run the spot until he or she hears it. You run the risk of costly make-goods by running spots thinking they're wonderful, only to find a mispronounced word running for a week.

When mistakes happen, offer a make-good after getting clearance from your manager. You now venture into the paperwork zone with credits. Try to stay away from your organization's business department at all costs. Someone up above sees you as part of the problem when paper with your name attached starts coming through.

In non-union shops, anyone can cut a spot. There might be times when you need to add your voice as a character in a spot, or possibly voice the entire announcement. Be careful. I've done voice work for twenty years, but shy away if I think the use of my voice will in any way hurt a campaign's chances for success.

In union shops, you'll probably never have the chance to be voice talent. You might also have a hard time cutting commercials in a hurry.

The production directors (PDs) at old-line stations run little fiefdoms that you enter cautiously. They often have contempt for the entire sales department, reveling in making you beg for production time to produce commercials that are the station's lifeblood.

PDs prefer doing more creative station promos. Can you blame them? The talent budget is higher, and the PDs greatly admire the famous voices who voice promos. Then *you* come in, wanting to change the Discount Hardwood Furniture August Sale spot.

AEs come and go; the production people are there for life. They see AEs as rude sorority girls who want action *now* and are always on deadline. When a spot is done, AEs grab it and rush to the client without the proper thanks and good-byes. Again, be aware of your support staff's feelings. Remember that they work harder for the same pay as you become more successful and make more money. Key word: Jealousy.

You can't win this battle. The only thing you can do is go back to the cold-calling techniques I keep alluding to, and work these people until they see you as one of the good AEs. Everybody likes somebody — it might as well be you.

When the spot is finally finished, make a copy for your client and one for yourself. If the client has five stores, have the production department make one for each store manager. They need to know what the spot sounds like, and exactly what product is being promoted. It is dangerous to assume that they are all fully aware of the current promotion.

Chapter Twenty-one

Producing a Local TV Spot

Most TV spots are thirty seconds rather than radio's sixty. It's amazing how much more can be crammed in to those thirty seconds because of the visual aspect.

If you work at a station with an expert camera crew, like I had at KOFY TV, much of the camera-angle work will be made easier for you. Whenever I took Bob Twig out on a shoot, the lighting, camera angles, and composition were perfect. A veteran TV producer, Bob taught me new tricks every time.

He was also great with clients. That's not always the case with cameramen who have limited understanding of station/client relations. A budding Spielberg, fully equipped with attitude, can spoil a shoot. When you have to deal with prima donnas, make sure you're prepared. Keep them fully informed of all developments, and show respect by asking for pre-shoot input.

The eye can take in at least *twelve images in thirty seconds*. Remember what I said in the mirroring session? Fifty-five percent of all information is taken in visually. That's why TV works so well. Visual images are easily remembered. Twelve might seem like too many cuts, but trust me: they'll make your spot better. A spot with only five or six shots has a slow-moving, amateurish look.

Script at least fifteen shots. You might not need them all, but that way, you'll make only one trip to a remote location. Prior to the shoot, go over shots with the camera people, so they bring proper equipment.

Never go to a shoot without lights. An outdoor desert shoot might morph into an indoor showroom opportunity. Be prepared.

Is it going to be miked or feature a voice-over? Know before you shoot.

Bring plenty of release forms. When you shoot inside a business, employees will line up to be in the spot. Usually, the cute ones will want to be part of the group. They must all sign releases to avoid possible problems later. Use as many staff members as possible. Feature gorgeous women prominently — they attract attention to the spot.

Each employee in the spot will tell his or her friends and totally buy into your campaign. You want them on your side in case the store sources leads. Do you think John's managers might give your station a couple of extra mentions on the source list if there's a vested interest in staying on TV?

It is especially important to include anyone who was skeptical of the TV idea in the first place. They're "taking their shoes off" when they allow themselves to be included in the spot. Remember my experience about customers recognizing me? It wasn't *me;* it was the power of *electronic media.* Staff-member recognition will increase personal sales figures.

Never come empty-handed. Bring a box of baked goods and some premium orange juice to the shoot. Pretend you're on a movie set. Sweets put everyone in a better frame of mind. Be sure to take care of your crew first. This is one of the best uses of expense account dollars — it's the coffeecake call all over again!

Acting!

Once, when I owned the shoe stores, I became involved in a high-profile political campaign. *The McNeil-Lehrer Report* came to my Palo Alto store to film a segment. As they set up the lights, the producer engaged me in conversation about my issue. The moment he thought I was sufficiently warmed up, he stepped out of the way and Charlayne Hunter Gault appeared. She asked me a couple of questions, which I answered spontaneously. Moments later they were gone.

One of my best friends, Robin Herman, saw the segment in Ohio and called to compliment me on how great I sounded. He was right. I sounded polished because a professional placed me in a comfortable state before a famous person asked the questions. I don't think I'd have done as well had I not been warmed up when Ms. Gault shoved the microphone in my face.

You used the coffeecake to break the ice at your first meeting. Use it again for the commercial shoot.

Expect several takes when the business owner speaks on camera. Ask John to *practice his lines at home* so he'll be smoother. It's usually better if John doesn't try to carry the whole spot — a break-in, like George Zimmer's "I guarantee it," works best.

Testimonials almost always pull. You need three or four to be credible. The business needs to offer satisfied customers some sort of honorarium to travel from home to the shoot. Use the same warm-up tactics I described above. Stand off-camera and ask open-ended questions. The satisfied customers need to sound natural. Know the key questions that will elicit the proper responses.

You're in charge here. Your usual obsequious approach with the client must change during the shoot. John expects you to be the expert. If you show uncertainty, his confidence might be shaken. Accepting suggestions is fine. Show strength. By your second shoot, you'll have more experience than anyone at Discount Hardwood Furniture has.

If you're unsure of the process, ask veteran camera operators at your station to take you to their next shoot as a helper. Bowing to their expertise will be educational, while also endearing you to the production mavens.

Look forward to shooting a commercial. They're usually fun. Your clients see you in a different light, further ingratiating you with them. And, it's a day away from phones and paperwork. No matter how difficult it is, remember: you're lucky to be there today.

Editing Your Commercial

Most stations now have digital editing suites. If your station still edits in analog, ask your GM when digital will arrive. Digital has made editing faster, more accurate, and more creative than the maddeningly tedious analog systems. Digital cameras are compact. Editing suites are tiny.

What's important to the AE is, you can bring your client into a small room with one editor and digitally craft a commercial in an hour or two. Don't like something? Zip — remove it. Whoops, changed my mind. Zip-zip — it's back.

Because digital editing is so precise, imperfections vanish. With new programs, more graphics can be added in fun ways. Discount Hardwood Furniture's spot can acquire a more national, network-quality feel. Film, of course, will still look better than video, but filming the spot adds thousands to its cost. Spend the money on frequency, instead.

The Musical Image

Ask clients if they've ever had a jingle produced for their business. If so, listen to it to determine whether it can be used for the current spot. A musical image is incredibly powerful.

I started at KOFY TV just as the jingle writers came to town. KOFY had signed with Jeff Archer's AVI Productions to produce musical-image campaigns for local retailers. My two managers, Mark Libby, LSM and Marc Artieres, RSM, were under the gun, because they'd made a big investment in AVI, and the current staff was having trouble making the program go.

AEs needed to convince local advertisers to attend a presentation at KOFY. Once there, each merchant met Jeff Arthur or his partner, Corey Reich, who discussed the prospect's business. Next, the prospect was given a twenty-minute station tour. Upon returning to the conference room, a catchy jingle was ready. Jeff or Corey sang it to the merchant, answered a few questions, then left. The AE, accompanied by a sales manager, then tried to close the deal for between $36,000 and $100,000.

The AVI program worked best when enough qualified prospects appeared. If fewer than the required number arrived, the station had to pay AVI a 20 percent commission on each deal, instead of 15 percent.

AVI is the kind of selling where *Conquering Cold-Calling Fear* techniques work perfectly. When someone asks me what's the best advice for jump-starting a sales career, my answer is, *"Make twenty calls a day."* Once you learn how much fun it can be, making twenty calls a day is no problem. With AVI, it took *forty* a day to get enough people to fill the schedule. No problem for me; *I wrote the book on cold calling.*

There was a contest to generate interest in the project. The first part of the contest was number of appointments. No problem — I doubled the number of the next-highest AE. Then came number of closes. I won that one, too. After only a few weeks at the station, an upstart with a radio background was showing up long-term AEs.

The musical-image campaigns were powerful. For a fraction of what it would have cost to hire local talent, nationally renowned musicians wrote and recorded memorable music proven to ring cash registers.

AVI was perfect for me. I remembered the jingle Steve Whiting wrote for Roots Natural Footwear in 1976, after he strolled into my store one day, plucking a guitar. It was fun and it worked. We produced a TV spot and ran it in San Jose during the length of the all-time-great *Roots* miniseries. That was the only time in its troubled history that my San Jose store was number one in the chain.

How great could it be for these local retailers to have someone with national-quality talent producing music for them! My first deal was with an auto-engine-replacement outfit called Dyno One, which I'd seen advertising on a competing station. Their hook was:

"It's the en...gine that makes *your car run... That's* why *there's Dyno One!"*

The music was great. The concept of the business was perfectly targeted to KOFY's pickup-truck-driving viewers. The spot was clean. I visited one day just as the spot ran, and saw all ten phone lines light up. Does it get any better than that for an AE?

A jingle will vastly improve your chance of success. It doesn't have to be perfect. It will be better than bland background music. If you're lucky enough to be associated with jingle writers, become their best friend. They'll put money in your pocket.

My relationship with Corey and Jeff at AVI became so close that I closed a deal by having them talk to my client over the phone, sans dog-and-pony show. The work was for a company called Golden Gate Plumbing and Rooter. Rick Gonzalez wanted his firm to be as memorable as Roto-Rooter. I told him the only way was through music. Then I had Jeff work up something and sing it over the phone from Miami. We closed a six-figure deal by Jeff singing:

"Golden Gate plumbing and Rooter... We keep your plumbing humming."

Rick liked the jingle so much that he had the hook printed on all his trucks. Golden Gate Plumbing's business went through the roof. He often said to me:

"Don, you're not just a salesman. I consider you more of a friend."

I bang on music because it sells. Anything that will give your client an edge must be used. If there's no jingle, *take the time to wade through as much music as necessary to set the perfect mood for the spot.* For going-out-of-business sales, the shouting announcer will be enough. In most other spots, read the script, so you can describe the mood to the production people before starting your search.

Graphics are the great time equalizer between TV and radio. You might not have to say the address or telephone number in a TV ad. Phrases like "Senior Citizen Discount" are perfect for a TV graphic. Each spoken word is so precious that graphics must be used. Folks can take it all in visually.

Be sure the style and color of the graphics match the tone of the spot. Your editor can help. He or she edits daily and understands what appeals to the eye. Also rely on you own instincts. You know the business better than the editor does. Seek your client's input here. This spot is her baby; it has to impress her friends and customers.

Editors are often overworked and may tend to rush you. Finish only when both the client and you are satisfied. That might necessitate another trip to the station, because a rushed spot turns out all wrong. You and your client must have the courage to make it as right as you can before it airs. When ready, get extra copies — and cross your fingers.

Chapter Twenty-two

Airing the Spot

Once the spot is ready, make sure your client receives the air times as soon as possible. In radio, it's usually a few days ahead; in TV, it's usually closer to the day of airing. Have your assistant fax the times every day for a while, so the client can be sure she and her friends see the spot. In the fax, remind her to send the times to all store managers. Some of those people starred in the spot, and will be especially interested in seeing the final version.

If your client gripes about spot placement, and you think the complaint is warranted, push your manager for an upgrade. Managers know how important proper placement is to new clients. When complaints are unreasonable, be prepared to defend the station and yourself.

Thank your assistant for faxing the times. He or she may have twenty-five time faxes to send out every day. The same techniques you use on client gatekeepers can be used in house.

Take the thank-you advice seriously. How many times have you gotten into hot water because you lacked concern for support staff feelings? *Unless you're a saint, there's probably someone at your station who hates you this minute.* You make twice as much as support staffers, and you eat expensive client lunches. No one watches over your time once you leave on sales calls. For all the support staffers know, you could be spending your days at the racetrack or attending movie matinees.

Ever hear the phrase "sales scum?" That's what they call us behind our backs — and sometimes in front. Most AEs shrug off the taunting. I turned to support staff on a couple of occasions and shot back:

"I'm proud of what I do for a living. How would you like it if I referred to you as 'production scum?'"

The answer, predictably, was, "Come on, Don. You know I was just kidding."

Sure. The same response you get when you call someone for making a racist, sexist, or anti-Semitic joke.

My response would be, "Great. I'm sure you don't really see me that way. Do you?"

"Oh, no. I wasn't referring to *you*"

The level of tension between sales and other departments often lies close to the surface. Protect your self-image, while taking pains to give the support staff respect.

Mirroring support staff can be as important as using the mirroring technique on prospects. It also helps to be courteous. Instead of saying:

"I need this typed by three o'clock today."

Say:

"Can you help me with an important project today? Is it possible to type this proposal by three this afternoon? The client demanded it, and I have to be out of the office until two."

It might seem like overkill, until you see the look on an assistant's face as you walk away after another seemingly unfair request. *Start memos with* please *and end them with* thank you. It takes an extra ten seconds to write and is incredibly well received by support staff.

Warning about Competitor Switch Pitches

It's good to check with your client the first week to see if the spot is O.K. Check also to insure that all store managers are aware of the campaign and the offer.

The phenomenon you need to prepare your client for in the next couple of weeks is the *incoming calls from your competitors trying to horn in on your success.* The inexperienced competitors will inform John how bad a fit Discount Hardwood Furniture is with WII FM. The smoother AEs will compliment him on choosing radio/TV/Cable and inquire about response.

Since it's too early to measure, they're starting to sow the seeds of doubt with John. Your job is to arm him with a comeback that will stop the calls. Have John tell your competitors:

"We're doing a four-for-one trade with WII FM; there's no cash involved. Does your station trade for prime-time spots?"

Checkmate!

The AE can go back to his manager and say, "Discount Hardwood has a trade deal." The manager will cross Discount Hardwood off his or her list of prospects, and the calls will stop. If John is uncomfortable with this little white lie, remind him that he might receive about ten calls from stations after his spots have aired. If John wishes to tell the whole truth, he can use your name and phone number as the person to contact.

The important issue here is that John is warned against your competition. If you fail to warn, you leave the door open for losing the account you worked so hard creating.

Warnings about Inflated Print Results

When businesses source leads, newspaper and Yellow Pages ads receive more than their fair share of acknowledgements. Blunt that problem before it starts, by asking your new client to be on the lookout for increased print and Yellow Pages response once electronic ads start to air. Before the schedule begins, ask John to monitor Yellow Pages response after your program starts.

I warned Rick, of Golden Gate Plumbing & Rooter, to check his *Yellow Pages* response when we went on the air. Rick noticed a marked increase. Now, when people looked for a plumber, they knew his name or saw the jingle with the musical notes in the ad. His response eclipsed other plumbers who had better page position in the book. That was one of the ways I was able to convince Rick that KOFY TV and, later, PAX TV, were working for him.

Calming Worried First-time Advertisers

Once the warnings are issued, your job with this client is done for a while. Early response to his ad will probably be spotty. New advertisers take time to enter the public consciousness. The more often you check for response, the greater the chance you'll worry your client. It's a good probability that the big push won't come until the fourth month, so relax.

The time for you to swing back into action is about six weeks down the road, when response has yet to come in and John starts worrying. The best way to keep him sane is to remind him of the success stories you mentioned during the sale. Retell George Zimmer's success in electronic media.

There's probably someone in your town who succeeds on TV. Cal Worthington Ford, Mr. Belvedere, and the Jewelry Exchange are all examples of successful independent electronic-media advertisers. Can you name one in your area? Write the name on an index card so you won't forget. Then use it to remind John to be patient.

Check for other problems. Make sure the commercial works. It might need to be tweaked. Bonus weight (extra free commercials) might be necessary to jack up response levels for a while. Show no fear. Calmly do what is necessary. Time will change response levels. The fourth month is almost always the turning point. Make sure John sticks with you at least until then.

If John says the campaign is not working, say:

"Really. Has business fallen off?" (Usually, it hasn't. Sales have increased; people simply didn't mention WII FM when they made purchases.)

"No, sales are actually up a little."

Ah-ha! Respond:

"So it's possible that WII FM is working, then?"

You're making John think like he normally does, with the bottom line in sight.

Keep probing. Ask about *Yellow Pages* response. Inexperienced salespeople often take a client's word for the failure of a campaign. When they report back to their managers, they become embarrassed when the managers ask the questions I mentioned here. Avoid such a trap. Ask your questions first.

Perhaps a competitive station has put impure thoughts in your new client's head. There may have been weather problems or bad economic news. When bad news was reported prominently during my retail days, it usually took a couple of weeks for the public to regain confidence and start buying again. Could that have been part of the problem? One of my clients on KABL AM went on the air during the week of 9-11-2001. Needless to say, the campaign is worth a try.

Before you admit defeat, make sure failure is due to WII FM's listeners not responding. You will lose many new clients. It's called *the churn*. A professional salesperson understands the phenomenon and never stops cold calling. For every success, there will be at least one failure, some because of a bad match, others a better offer, still others when you absolutely cannot convince the client to stay with you until the campaign succeeds. Keep making your cold calls and the churn will not cause you major problems.

Chapter Twenty-three

It's Working! What Now?

When the program starts to take off, make sure John knows his success is a direct result of your station and yourself. *Blame for failure of John's campaign will be yours alone, so you must take credit for success.* Now is not the time for false modesty! It *is* a good time to add those extra months John was reluctant to commit to at the beginning.

Add on when John is satisfied. A show of satisfaction is rare. When he comes to his senses, he'll be a tougher negotiator. Work on him now. Say:

"John, why not lock in these rates until the end of the year? The station's ratings are climbing. If we renegotiate nearer fourth quarter, my manager will be greedier. Now he's a little desperate. It's easier to just extend the contract; if it lapses for one day, I have to have a new contract approved all over again. You know how managers can be."

Always pitch when the client is in a buying mood. In the shoe business, the adding-on technique would have resulted in a perfectly matched purse or some shoe polish to go along with the new shoes. Here, it's continuing a contract that now will become an annual.

Keeping Annual Accounts Happy

You did it! Discount Hardwood Furniture is now an annual client. It's much easier to keep a satisfied client than find a new one. Start with an expensive lunch celebration. Ask John which is his favorite restaurant. If he doesn't have an answer, ask what kind of food he likes. Set a date and make reservations.

Always suggest lunch! Female AEs have all had the experience of offering lunch and having the car dealer client try to change it to dinner. Dinner is appropriate for large station functions or annual holiday parties. Fancy dinners with a couple of large clients and more than one station person can become memorable events. Dinners with new clients are usually inappropriate, tend to be awkward, and extend your workday.

Recently many large radio conglomerates took away AE expense accounts. Now lunches must include managers. Do the lunch anyway. You will show off the success of your new client to your boss — your number one client.

Become the Happy Ticket Broker

The next step is game tickets. Most stations in major markets have tickets for the local baseball team. Basketball, hockey, and football tickets are harder to find. Value increases with the lack of availability.

Abbott Supply Company always had eight season tickets to the Detroit Lions football team. M. H. and I went to a few games; the rest were for clients. I remember seeing Pop in action. With a set of tickets sitting on his desk, he'd call a client and say:

"I might be able to locate a couple of tickets to the Lions-Packers game on Sunday. Will you be available?"

If the client said he wanted the tickets, Pop would reply:

"Will you be there this afternoon? I'll call you back if I can get 'em."

When he called back several hours later, he had squeezed

every possible ounce of value from those tickets.

Your station might have access to rock concert, ballet, opera, or movie tickets. Whatever's available, snag at least your fair share and start calling. Common wisdom says don't ask at a late date. I disagree. Merely say:

"These tickets just landed on my desk fifteen minutes ago. I know it's last minute, but are you free to see Madonna tonight?"

It matters little if they can go. You earn recognition for thinking of a client at a time when you have nothing to sell. Damn! This is nothing but a good deed. Who can not like that?

Acting!

Last-minute invitations are among my favorites, especially if the event is highly prized. I might call seven clients before finding a taker. The other six remember what I tried to do for them. The next time I call, do you think they might be a little more eager to answer the phone?

At KKSF I was the only man on the sales staff. Baseball tickets became my specialty. Everyone accepted my calls. Movie posters are perfect for clients with kids. Anything kid-related gives the client something to do with his or her family, and helps cement your relationship.

One of my best giveaways was to a client who was bringing his family of four from Sacramento to San Francisco for the weekend. I sent them Museum of Modern Art passes and a voucher to a high-class pizza restaurant near their hotel. My contribution made their trip a success. Shortly thereafter, I received a surprise annual order.

You're doing a good deed by calling and offering tickets — there's no begging for business involved. Those extra contacts set you apart from the typical self-serving AE who only has time for a client when a buy is up. Buyers resent that kind of treatment.

If many tickets are available, be sure your favorite gatekeepers have a chance at the freebies. Next come your personal assistant, traffic department, production department, and business manager. Don't tell anyone you have tickets until you know the tickets are available. Remember the jealousy factor.

Whenever possible, accompany your client to the game. If you absolutely can't stand baseball or the opera, pick something you can handle. When you must accompany the client to an event you hate, go out for refreshments and check your voice mail from time to time. They key issue is establishing a closer relationship with your client.

It's easier for a man to take a male client to a ball game, and for a woman to accompany a female client to the symphony. Never give the impression that the event is anything more than business. Nothing is worse than having clients think you're coming on to them.

A great way to preclude possible feelings of harassment is to find four tickets, and invite the client and his or her mate to join you and your significant other for an event. Another way is to use the same four tickets to bring three separate clients. Competing shoe-store owners — no! Complementary businesses, such as plumbers and contractors, work better together.

While your first priority in ticket giveaway is loyal clients, occasionally there's one who has yet to buy for legitimate reasons. Offer this prospect some last-minute tickets. It will open her up a bit and make it easier when she's are ready to purchase your product.

Occasionally, clients have a company policy against accepting anything. Fine. You should have found this out during your first face to face, when you brought in the coffeecake. You know now, so you can cross him off your preferred guest list.

Clients who regularly accept gifts are generally easier to control than those who refuse them. The *refuseniks* will want to judge you totally on performance. The acceptors will often allow for a mistake or two along the way without dire consequences.

I'm disappointed when any salesperson brags about never going over his or her entertainment budget. That's the best money
you can spend, so spend every dime and push management for
extras. Every non-pressure contact you make with a client brings
you closer to consultant status. Every unused free movie pass
costs you potential clients, and takes food out of your children's
mouths.

Put down the book and make four calls today to give away
something. List the results on a separate sheet of paper, using this
simple format:

Client: *John Smith*

Gift: *Theater tickets*

Benefit: *Consultancy*

Chapter Twenty-four

Cracking Your First Big Agencies

You've shown the ability to generate new business. A senior AE leaves your station and you're awarded your first agency account. It will probably be a small-to-midsize agency that's already doing business with the station. Your job is to keep the agency buying while you become established with the buyer.

There are always stations not getting on buys in radio. When a popular AE leaves a mid-level station, the buyer often zips the replacement for a while until the new AE is broken in. There's always a station waiting in the wings whose ratings or promotions weren't good enough to make the buy. That station's AE might have been trying for a year to break the ice. Now his or her turn arrives.

You must consider the buyer at your new agency like the decision-maker you tried to reach by cold calling. The same tactic of becoming the gatekeeper's, then the assistant's, best friend works here.

You won't have as hard a time reaching the buyer, because her job is to talk to folks like you. The difference is, she'll cut you a new butt-hole if you're not careful. She knows how much money she controls, and already has a set-in-stone opinion about your station. She won't be as easily swayed by mirroring and will control the first meeting.

She'll want to size you up to see whether you know your business. Know everything about your station before your visit. She will listen to *new* information, so don't waste her time with the basic station rap. She hates to break in new AEs. She's been there for ten years and is sick of people like you — a new AE shows up from your station every year; just when that person is broken in, here you come. You'd better entertain her or expect a hard time.

This media queen might be interested when you have good gossip. She needs a full overview of the market, so if you become a source of new information, you'll be more welcome. The last order of business in Karen Hodges' sales meetings at KTVU was: "Any news in the market this week?"

That was a great opportunity to share news that could be quickly relayed to agency buyers.

Your new media queen is also used to receiving freebies. Bringing in great tickets on your first visit is a good start. Let her know you'll be a conduit for good things. Talk about the station in general terms. Get to know her. You need to find out:

(*How she likes her proposals written;*

(*Whether her agency uses Cost-Per-Point or Cost-Per-Thousand;*

(*What information it's important to send;*

(*Her favorite sports and activities;*

(*All the accounts she handles. This isn't always easy; she might not want you to know about all of them, because she has no intention of buying your station for those accounts.*

Some new *big* agencies need to be given ticket offers before you get on any buys. Agency media queens despise AEs who call only when business is up. By staying in contact, you'll immediately gain ground on the self-serving dilettantes who work for your competition.

When a client asks you for a bid on an upcoming ad campaign (an "avail request"), meet with your manager to plot a strategy before submitting your proposal. Each station has a different philosophy. At KKSF we always came in above the suggested cost per point. Because we ran only nine commercials an hour, instead of twelve like our competitors, we felt that each one was more valuable because it had a better chance of being heard.

If you're not clear on what the buyer wants, write out questions. Then call the buyer to find answers before you submit a proposal. If the deadline is impossible to reach, call to ask for an extension. Buyers will almost always grant you an extra day. Never turn anything in late without permission. The other stations submitted on time. Tardiness provides an excuse for the buyer to zip you.

Many agencies will demand a guarantee on ratings that you offer for TV buys. When your ratings fail to reach the agreed-upon levels, they'll expect *bonus weight* (free commercials). Those promises can cause unnecessary, time-consuming paperwork. Some managers would rather give bonus weight by over-promising to get on a buy. They don't have to do the paperwork called *posting*, which determines how much needs to be made up. Whether they like it or not, managers almost always agree to bonus weight to stay in major agencies' good graces.

It's better for you to come in with realistic numbers and lower the rate a bit than have to fret about performance over the length of the contract. If you're lucky, an assistant will post for you. If not, you'll need to work late checking the overnight ratings for problem areas. Why not come in with realistic numbers and avoid those kinds of problems?

When you establish trust, provide useful information, come through with good rates, and make good on your ratings estimates, you'll be on the road to acceptance. Now you can ask the buyer to lunch. Buyers will accept only when you've proven yourself. They've been wined and dined everywhere, so use your restaurant trade only if it can't be avoided. Take them to the best places, especially if your manager is paying. Keep in mind that they might make less money than salespeople, often work very hard, and rely on freebies for a higher standard of living.

When you fail to make it on a buy, your manager will want to know the reasons. Keep the same tone you adopted with the buyer when you were schmoozing her. Ask her nicely:

"What can I do better to get on the next buy?"

Or:

"Where did I need to be on this buy? My manager will need to know."

Have the answer before the question is asked. Often, the manager gave you rates that weren't competitive. You'll be armed against the possible coming managerial abuse.

If you considered the buyer your new best friend and then whined when you were zipped, she'll see through you for the phony you've become. Keep an even countenance or you could lose the next round too.

Media queens who seem so tough when you first walk in can be the most fun people on your list. They need to break you in to be an effective agency person. When you succeed, they can be fun and profitable.

Chapter Twenty-five

The Cancellation Turtle

Some sales campaigns end in failure. It happens to all of us. The cancellation of an annual contract after three months hurts worse than never having gotten the deal. The figures have already shown on your printout; you might have spent the money; it could cost you a quarterly bonus—none of these outcomes are good.

Here's a wonderful temporary solution. Many years ago, I received a large cancellation at KFRC. I went for a walk and found myself at the Rocky Mountain Chocolate Factory in the San Francisco's Embarcadero Center. There I saw the biggest chocolate turtle in history, and I bought it for my return to the station.

As I walked in the door munching my sweet treat, an experienced AE named Ann Lee McGurk approached me and said, "Oh, you bought the cancellation turtle! What happened?"

My mood changed instantly. It hit me that we all suffered miserable experiences. I wasn't the first, nor would I be the last one to drown my sorrows in chocolate. Ann Lee validated my sorrow and already knew the quick solution.

The cancellation turtle has become a part of my repertoire. When I have a big cancellation, or a client trashes me, I take a break and look for a chocolate turtle. The little reward when that happens reduces the hurt to bite-sized pieces that can be handled much more easily.

Try it. When something bad happens, take a break. Treat yourself to a special pleasure. When you return to your desk, the misery will have partially subsided, and you'll be able to concentrate on making up those lost dollars — today.

Bad News — An Outcome Rather than a Downer

I admit to not being the most emotionally stable person in media. I've been known to smash the phone down several times after particularly disappointing calls. Three phones died unnatural deaths at KOFY TV alone. That's why I feel qualified to lecture on ways to overcome anger and disappointment at the station. If you never become upset over things going wrong, you might not be trying hard enough to succeed. When a prospect says:

"You're a great salesman, but I'm not buying. Don't take it personally," you had better take it personally!

If you were a great salesperson, you would have made the sale. You *should* take it personally. Your manager will. He or she wants you returning with orders, not explanations.

When someone gives me the "Don't take it personally" line, I reply:

"That's what my high school sweetheart told me when she gave back my letter sweater. I still felt horrible."

If your relationship is strong, the buyer might find a way to get you on a buy. It happens all the time in agency buys. By not saying it's O.K. and implying that it's *not*, you stand a better chance of getting on the next round. The prospect now knows that it hurts you to lose a sale without your having to lose respect by whining.

Here are a couple of positive activities you can engage in when you feel terrible:

(*Take a walk and buy your favorite sweet thing.*

(*Clean your desk.*

This echoes the advice I received when I first took over Abbott Chemical at age twenty-two. I went to a Small Business Administration (SBA) assistance group that assigned me an accountant to help make sense of Abbott's cloudy financial picture. We had several fruitful discussions on operational procedures, which helped me straighten out Abbott's problems and make it a viable business for my folks again.

Mark, seeing my frustration, offered the piece of wisdom I remember best:

"When in doubt, clean up."

I've been cleaning up for many years.

Can't figure out what to do next? Having a bad day? Clean your desk. File those contracts sitting in your OUT basket. Send that half-finished thank-you note on your desk. You'll have accomplished something without having your bad vibes ruin a budding relationship with a new client.

When things start going badly, it helps sometimes to shut up for a while. If you're like me, there's always something to do around your desk. Take an hour and clean up. You'll feel better, because the time you've taken to clean up allowed you time to process the hurt.

Get back on the phone!

Have you made your twenty calls today? Now is the time to make them. Don't start with the toughest person to reach. Begin by calling good clients who won't beat you up. Pay them a courtesy call. Think of a reason to phone: new ratings stories, ticket giveaways, perhaps asking about a vacation.

Start by doing a good deed. Wipe away the bad by doing someone good. As you start feeling better, the calls can become more serious. It's O.K. if all the calls are puffy, but please try not to say:

"Hi, Jane. Just checking in!"

That phrase bugs some buyers. They have no time for idle chatter, so give them something. It will pay off.

It's amazing how often you can return to the phones and, before the day ends, make up in sales what you lost earlier in the day. You're in a state of heightened awareness after a big hurt. Clients seem to respond to that sense of urgency *only* if you don't start by feeling sorry for yourself.

Don't feel sorry for yourself. Nobody wants to buy from a loser. Keep the big hurt to yourself. Clients want confidence. It rubs off easily. That's why you don't have to ask for orders today. It's the wrong time to beg, so talk, instead.

When in Doubt — Do Nothing!

What I mean by that is when you are not sure what to do because of a setback, try not to make any major decisions. They inevitably will not turn out the way you hope.

If you've had a setback and are also trying to close a big deal today, wait till you feel better. A call right away will probably cost you the deal. After your twenty calls are done and some positive energy flows, then you can begin thinking about that big deal.

Chapter Twenty-six

Collecting Every Dime on Time

Remember earlier when I said to look right in clients' eyes when you asked about their credit? I did that so you could find out who's naughty or nice before problems start.

How I handle the credit end of the account depends on how my new client answers. People with great credit don't hesitate to brag. Folks with problems would rather not have anyone check on them.

What you say to your credit department will give them direction. I have never been wrong about someone whose credit I personally O.K.'d to the credit department. Everyone is fooled occasionally; I've been wrong on businesses I *hoped* would be good. Those were accounts I closed when I desperately needed billing and asked too few questions. Down deep, I knew they were trouble.

After a while I wearied of chasing down deadbeats. When I closed a new account that was shaky, credit was never mentioned. I assumed cash up front for everything. If they asked for credit I simply said:

"We always start new business clients on a cash-in-advance (CIA) basis, because of the outlay necessary to set up new accounts. We'll gladly let you fill out a credit application, but we find that pay-as-you-go seems to work best for new advertisers."

That usually garners at least some cash up front.

The problem with CIA clients is, you wind up paying a monthly visit to pick up a check. No matter how great it is to see your clients regularly, once a month visits mean your annual contract is only as good as the previous month's business.

What about good clients who fall on hard times? How do you make sure you don't wind up with charge-backs? The business department hates charge-backs. Collection percentage is often part of their bonus structure. Want to get them to dislike you quickly? Have a couple of large clients go belly up.

I've had some business managers I was happy to sic on dead-beats. Others, I refused any contact with my clients. Find out *today* the policy at your station, and be the one AE who follows it perfectly.

Your goal is to have as little contact with the business department as possible. The more time you spend there explaining your errors, the less time you have to close new business. Also, your manager hates to hear the business department complain. When you're the one they're after, it costs you valuable points with the person you need to impress most in your business life. Why take that chance?

Over the years, I've been known as the guy who can clean up departed AEs' financial messes. These often result in someone leaving before bad paper rains down, revealing either bogus or shaky contracts.

When I first started at KFRC, I collected a previous AE's huge overdue account by taking frequent 130-mile trips to Sacramento. It was hard to say no with me leaning over someone's desk — a technique I learned at Abbott Supply.

Post-riot Detroit's tough business climate led to Abbott's long dive from a thirty-five-year-old profitable janitorial-supply business to one on the brink of bankruptcy. I was summoned from my career as an inner-city junior high school teacher to try to save the business.

One of my first tasks was to collect every dime people owed us. We had a client who ran a doctor's office. They had over-ordered supplies, thinking we would go out of business and never be able to collect. I asked two of my East Side pals pay Roger a visit.

Peter Lumetta, who would later become my partner in the shoe business, used to entertain us by tearing thick telephone books in half. Ron Buck was a former football player of large stature. As they entered the doctor's office, Buck stood at the door and Peter asked for the check.

An emergency phone call came to Abbott from Roger:

"Don, did you send these goons to kick my ass?"

I put my sister Alice on the line to listen, since Roger had been best man at her wedding. My reply was:

"Roger, we just want the money. Can you pay today, please."

Alice added:

"I was listening. Don never threatened to *kick your ass.*"

Roger gave Peter and Buck the check, but Peter wasn't through. He got on the phone and asked me if he could take a check. Our little game had gone far enough; I said yes.

O.K., you don't have to threaten people to collect money. The opposite way of collecting generally works better.

During the shoe-store years, there were times when I was a tad late paying bills.

One legitimate reason for not paying a bill was a dispute over merchandise. Nordstrom could send back for full credit any shoe not to their liking. As a small operator I was never allowed that option. The only way for a small merchant like me to earn what's called "markdown money" in the trade was to withhold payment.

I only withheld payment for good reasons. When the collection department called, I would calmly state my case and ask for relief. It was usually no more than 25 percent of the bill. After a couple of phone calls, we'd cut some sort of deal and I'd pay the bill that day.

The heavy-handed shoe companies got on the phone and threatened legal action. I told them I'd see them in court. I knew what would happen next: First I would never do business with that company again; second, another month would go by before the lawyer contacted me.

As soon as the lawyer's letter arrived, I'd give him a call and explain my side of the story. Then we'd negotiate a reasonable settlement, which he would bring back to the company and sell to them. It was to the lawyer's benefit to settle after one letter and one short phone call. He'd get half of what he collected that day without ever getting his hair mussed.

The only loser was the self-righteous shoe manufacturer.

Bottom line: If you bring in the lawyers, the client wins. *Never threaten!*

The best collectors I ever met did to me exactly what I've been telling you to do with your clients: they established a relationship with me, so I would always pay them first.

The woman from Zodiac Shoes was the best. She had me send her a picture of my baby daughter for her desk. Think I tried extra hard to pay Zodiac on time? You bet!

You must collect the money before it's permanently lost. Work your aging list like your lead list. The bookkeepers of deadbeat companies must become your newest best friends. Yours isn't the only organization these slow-pay clients aren't paying. Get to the front of the line by *Conquering Cold-Calling Fear.*

An additional problem is that media bills are often paid last, especially when the client has no plans to use you again. They'll always pay their important suppliers first. In order to jump to the head of the line, you must work hard.

A great time for collection calls is while you're cleaning up after a tough day. I find it slightly refreshing to be a touch more aggressive when I'm in a bad mood. Don't think of it as taking revenge for all the pain someone else has caused you today. Simply realize that you're in a better frame of mind to collect when you're slightly out of sorts. See how much better you feel after making a couple of collection calls on an otherwise bleak day.

Be nice! And be persistent. It's not unlike fogging. Make each call positive. If someone says he'll put the check in the mail today and you don't believe him, offer to come and pick it up, using the same line you used to set the appointment:

"I'm going to be in your area this afternoon. How about I swing by and pick it up. It'll save you a stamp."

The swing-by works with honest people. Deadbeats know that trick and say, "No, I'd rather send it." When they say they're sending, ask for the check number. You might force them to make out the check early.

Many clients have no idea that you'll lose your commission if they fail to pay within ninety days. You must explain that you, their new best friend, will have worked for free if payment doesn't arrive by month's end.

An attractive leather bag saleswoman once gave me the "I'll lose my commission" rap, so I offered to pay her the commission only. Her answer was:

"Grow up, Don! Pay the whole amount right now!"

I sheepishly complied, after which we had lunch at her house and became better friends.

For people who you know won't pay unless you stand over them while they write the check, you must surprise them. Often these sneaks hide behind voice mail. When confronted, they pay up. The tactic has worked often for me.

Be careful whom it is you're visiting. If you think someone might pose a threat to your safety, take one of the other AEs or a manager. Granted, I make collections in California. Nobody ever pulled a gun on me here. In fact, if I think I might have trouble down the line with a client, I *mention* that I grew up in Detroit. The word Detroit seems to intimidate some people.

That tactic was unsuccessful with a siding company I mistakenly got on the air in my early radio days. When they failed to pay, and stopped returning my phone calls, I started showing up unannounced. Each time I arrived, a different wise guy was in charge. Finally, I talked to their lawyer in Indianapolis. After an informative discussion, I decided the healthy decision would be to give up quickly.

Finally, the day you lose the commissions, stop wasting your time on deadbeats. Unless you can convince the station to pay you a commission on what you collect, it's time to move on.

Chapter Twenty-seven

Kissing your Boss' Butt Correctly

As a successful AE, you start by kissing your boss' butt. Next, you travel to the prospect's gatekeeper. From the gatekeeper, your lips seek the prospect, whom you turn into a butterfly of a client by careful butt kissing. You might next have to kiss your assistant's behind for help with a proposal.

When you return with the order, you kiss your manager's butt to have the station accept your low rates. Then you start with support staff: traffic, business, and production; fail to kiss those butts and your days in the office are no fun.

Did I forget anyone? Oh, yes — your receptionist. Kiss her butt properly and you might snag an extra call-in lead from time to time.

Now that you've become accomplished at butt kissing, you're a successful AE ready to meet the world. If you kiss butt the way you've always done it, butt kissing becomes hard work. Use mirroring, the 70/30 Rule, listening better and concentrating on "you" instead of "me," and you'll accomplish the same result without the bad aftertaste.

Who's the most important person in your business life? That's right, your manager! Even when he asks you to do something you know to be kindergarten work, say yes.

Why? Because there are several other AEs, and you know a

couple of them will start whining immediately. A couple of others will simply refuse the task.

Outrageous tasks have a way of dying a natural death. You be the one who turns in the odious work once. When all the others fail, you'll have added more dollars to your psychic checkbook. You'll need every dollar later.

Manager has a special package you know is awful? Simply send out a one-sheet to your contact list. It's easily done with the help of your assistant. The bad pitch is out. You've made a non-intrusive connection. Who knows? Your good deed might bring surprise business.

I average about 100 clients on my list. A client mailer usually achieves a 2–3 percent return. More importantly, I make contact again.

You've done the deed. Your manager continues to consider you a team player. When you want to be given that big agency list that's come up because a senior AE left, spend the psychic dollars in your checkbook. Request the plum! You'll probably score.

At the end of the month, when the manager needs $5000 to make budget, you be the one to spend two hours dialing for dollars. If you've established a consultancy position with your core clients, you can go to them with a pants-down deal and close it before month's end.

Obviously, you can't do that with the same people all the time. I've always had a few bottom feeders whom I can call with a lowball deal at the last minute to get me out of a jam. When you become a successful AE with good rates, those once-in-a-while lowball deals will be accepted. You'll be the savior.

Chapter Twenty-eight

The Hat Man

When I informed one of my all-time favorite clients, Mike Baddley, of Seraphein Beyn in Sacramento, that I had written a book on sales, he asked me if I'd included a chapter on my hats. It occurred to me that I'd forgotten one of the secrets of my success. So, Mike, this chapter is dedicated to you, a charter member of the follically challenged hat-man fan club.

I was the first guy on my block to start losing my hair. By the time I was in grad school, the comb-over nonsense stopped, and the fact that I was bald, like my lovable Pappy Smith and Uncle Dave, was a fact. A bald head can get awfully cold in Michigan winters, so I started wearing hats.

One of my favorites was a cowboy hat I wore every day when I taught at Sherrard Junior High School in Detroit's inner city. The students had nicknames for every teacher. My long curly hair, cowboy boots, and favorite hat generated the nickname "Custer." Had I walked around hatless, something awful — like "baldy" — might have been my moniker. That was my first success as a hat wearer.

Fast-forward through many careers to my start in radio sales. I began at legendary KFRC AM in San Francisco. The station was located on the city's windiest corner. My bald head took a pounding until I started wearing felt hats. They were the only hats I could wear with the suits and sport coats necessary in that sales position.

It soon became apparent that I was an oddity — a man with a hat in an otherwise hatless San Francisco business world. The response was immediate and positive. Almost every day, someone would compliment my hat with a statement like:

"Great hat! Why don't men wear hats anymore?"

It occurred to me that I was unique, so I continued wearing hats even when the weather improved.

Roger Becker, owner of a small ad agency, started calling me "the Hat Man." Whenever anyone in the Bay Area radio world heard that phrase, they knew it referred to Don Surath. I quickly become well known, so much so that on one occasion, I totally overshadowed a beauty queen.

As KFRC sales manager, I took a beautiful young saleswoman who claimed to be the former Miss Georgia on a sales call to the *Asian Yellow Pages.* We had a good meeting and she eventually closed a piece of business with them. Six years later, on a sales call for WB20 TV, I paid a visit to the *Chinese Yellow Pages.*

The gentleman I visited looked familiar. After a while, I asked him if he was the same guy who used to buy advertising for the *Asian Yellow Pages.* Then it hit him — he remembered me.

He asked, "You're the guy with the hat, aren't you?

"That's me," I answered.

"I thought you'd remember the blonde beauty I was with, the former Miss Georgia."

"No, sorry. I only remember you," he replied, much to my astonishment, making my day in the process.

Once I started working for WB20, the need for hats practically disappeared. Parking was available directly in front of the building in the warmest part of San Francisco. I stopped wearing hats unless it was raining.

Now I have another problem: buyers who've known me for years look forward to my hat collection. When I show up hatless, they feel cheated. What's a guy to do? I have to keep notes on who needs to see me in a hat and who doesn't care.

One of my favorite hat techniques is to wear an expensive wool overcoat with the hat, and look like I came from central casting for a 40s gangster movie. Most clients either love the look or are slightly intimidated. Either reaction works for me. The gangster look works especially well on collection calls. A large cell phone in the inside left pocket doesn't hurt.

When Ed Krampf wanted to hire me at Clear Channel to sell KABL AM last year, he first asked about the hats. When I came to the interview hatless, he was disappointed. After being at KABL for a month, there was a company-wide sales outing at a local club. The room was hot, so I stashed my hat. When Ed introduced me and I stood up bareheaded, he asked for the hat. I had to run over to the other side of the room to wave it for my new colleagues.

What does this all mean? It means that as "the Hat Man" I've become a known quantity in my field. Luckily, the impression has so far been positive. With over fifty stations competing for business in the crowded Bay Area radio market, standing out in the crowd is a good thing.

Do I recommend wearing a hat to work? Not if it doesn't suit you. Should you be known for something? Yes! David Greenwald was known as "the Muffin Man" for many years. On a regular basis, he stopped in unannounced with muffins for his good customers. Our real estate agent, Sarah Southwick, wears unique outfits and sexy high heels every day. Other agents try to be conservatively tasteful. Sara sells rings around them by being unique and having fun in the process.

Whether it's coffeecake, muffins, great shoes, red lipstick, or bagels, being known for something positive will make selling easier and more fun. Think of something you can use. It will be fun for you, and help you become a known quantity in your field.

Overview

You tried the effortless selling method, *Conquering Cold-Calling Fear,* at the beginning of the book. Answer the following questions honestly.

(*Did you do the 100 leads?*

(*Have you been making twenty calls a day?*

(*Has your relationship with gatekeepers improved?*

(*Are you closing more deals?*

(*Has your internal situation improved?*

(*Are you dealing with negative outcomes more gracefully?*

(*How has your relationship with your manager changed?*

(*Are you happier selling with more technique and less effort?*

(*Have you successfully broken into some agencies?*

(*Are you collecting every dime on time?*

Use this page as a marker for your progress. If you've answered no to any of these questions, go back to the appropriate chapter, re-read it, and do what it says. Merely reading *Conquering Cold-Calling Fear* will not accomplish your goals — you must practice the techniques while they're fresh in your mind.

Keep me informed of your progress. E-mail me at yfds@pacbell.net and share your successes. I'll be here to help. Check the Web site for future seminars and available products. Keep this book as your reference guide. I've added a bibliography of important resources. Contact them for more help.

Go to seminars whenever they're offered. I learn more about selling every time I interact with an audience. When you participate, you'll help and be helped.

Have you given any thought to the answer to my hardware storeowner's request?

"One word."

It took me years to realize the answer. You won't be placed in that situation if you use *Conquering Cold-Calling Fear* techniques properly, so there's no need to come up with an answer. But, in case you thought it over and have one, send your answer to my Web site, and I'll publish it in the next newsletter.

Finally, you are a performer. Perform for your clients. They want to be entertained. Don't tell yourself, "I can't do this. It's silly."

Try out the silly stuff. You might find it to your liking. Make a pact with yourself to try my method:

P.A.C.T.

Patience, Acting Courage, Technique

Bibliography

Allen, Jeffrey G. *Jeff Allen's Best: Win the Job.* New York: John Wiley & Sons, 1990.

Beckman, Nicholas. *How To Make People Like You In 90 Seconds or Less.* New York: Workman Publishing Company, Inc., 2000.

Friedman, Harry J. *Successful Retail Selling.* Los Angeles: National Retail Workshops, 1985.

Griffin, Jack. *How to Say it Best.* Paramus, NJ: Prentice Hall, 1994.

Halberstam, David. *Playing for Keeps: Michael Jordan and the World He Made.* New York: Random House, 1999.

Jennings, Jason. *Quantum New Business Development* Video Training Program. Dallas, TX: AVI Communications, Inc., 1997.

King, Larry. *How to Talk to Anyone, Anytime, Anywhere.* New York: Crown Publishers, Inc., 1994.

King, Steven. *On Writing.* New York: Scribner, 2000.

Kushner, Malcolm. *Successful Presentations for Dummies.* Foster City, CA: IDG Books Worldwide, 1996.

LeNoble, Dr. Philip J. *System 21.* Littleton, CO: Executive Decision Systems, 1984.

LeNoble, Dr. Philip J. *Retail In$ights* monthly. Executive Decision Systems, 2002.

Robbins, Anthony. *Unlimited Power* Audio Tapes. Chicago: Nightingale Conant, 1986.

Sandler, David. *You Can't Teach A Kid to Ride A Bike at A Seminar, The Sandler System.* Stevenson, MD: Bay Head Publishing, 1999.

Schiffman, Steven. *Cold Calling Techniques That Really Work.* Holbrook, MA: Adams Media Corporation, 1999.

Weiss, Wendy. *Cold Calling For Women: Opening Doors & Closing Sales.* New York: D.F.D. Publications, 2000.